KONSTANTY
BUSZCZYŃSKI

Impressions of America

Second Expanded Edition

With a Supplementary Outline
of the History of the United States

Translated by Kasia Beresford

KABATY
PRESS

KABATY PRESS
Published by Kabaty Press, Warsaw
www.kabatypress.com

Editing and Project Management by Isobelle Clare Fabian

ISBN Paperback 978-83-955562-0-3
ISBN ePub 978-83-955562-1-0
ISBN Mobi 978-83-955562-2-7
ISBN PDF 978-83-955562-3-4

Interior Design by Michael Grossman

Table of Contents

Foreword
by Dominic A. Pacyga

From the nineteenth until the early twentieth century several Polish intellectuals visited the United States and wrote about what they had seen. Perhaps the most famous account is Henryk Sienkiewicz's *Letters from America*, which were serialized in various Polish journals from 1876-1879. Professor Emil Habdank Dunikowski came twice to the United States to explore the American Polonia and find out its relationship to the Polish lands. Dunikowski eventually convinced Chicago's Polish leadership to take part in the Lwów Provincial Fair of 1894. He wrote *Wśrod Polonii w Ameryce (Among the Poles in America)* in 1893. Other Poles also published their impressions of America. In the Polish lands, and particularly in Austrian occupied Galicia, many Polish intellectuals were interested in the relationship of the vast *Za Chlebem* or economic emigration that took place roughly from 1855 until the mid-1920s. This large migration of Polish peasants from the rural areas of Poland to the United States concerned those who hoped the peasantry would help to save Poland and resurrect it on the political map of Europe. Konstanty Buszczyński's *Impressions of America* fits well into this tradition. This short book was written more than 100 years ago as Europe found itself entangled in the Great War that saw Poland re-merge as an independent nation. Buszczyński depicts the United States as the future of Western Civilization. Even if seen from the point of view of the times, the author certainly paints a rather overly enthusiastic picture of the United States. He even admits that he might be accused of too positive a bias toward America.

Buszczyński, the son of Stefan and Helena (Hlebicki-Józefowicz) Buszczyński married Jadwiga Dmochowska with whom he had six children. As a young man, he graduated from the Real School in Dresden, Germany and began his studies at the Dresden University of Technology. He soon moved to the Riga University of Technology in the Russian Empire. Buszczyński studied briefly at the Faculty of Chemistry (1877-1878) and afterwards attended the University of Lwów in Galicia. He returned to the Riga University of Technology and its Faculty of Agriculture, where he obtained a diploma with distinction in 1883. After graduation, he worked at his estate in Niemiercze in Podolia, and in 1886 started a business focused on development and production of sugar beet seeds with his relative Łążyński. In 1894 Łążyński sold his share of the business to Buszczyński, who expanded the business substantially and became a market leader in research and development of seed varieties. His company eventually owned research and development facilities in both California and Utah, which were used for testing the performance of various seeds under specific climactic conditions. He spent much of his time during 1910-1912 in the United States, and drew on this for the first edition of *Impressions of America* in 1916. Due to this experience, Minister Leon Wasilewski entrusted him with organizing the first Polish consulate in New York City, where he served as consul general

(1919). Buszczyński was dismissed from the post by Prime Minister Ignacy Jan Paderewski for participating in the congress of the National Defense Committee, a group supporting Józef Piłsudski in Boston. Before his death in 1921 he returned to Poland and was buried in the Rakowicki Cemetery in Kraków. This second edition of *Impressions of America* was published after his death in 1922.

This travel memoir is based on his visits to the United States in 1910 and 1912 before the cataclysm that would engulf Europe in the summer of 1914. Originally published in 1916 in Kraków, as war raged across the Polish lands, it is a love song to the nation he had visited a few years earlier. This second edition appeared after the entrance of the United States into the war. Buszczyński lauds President Woodrow Wilson's speech outlining what he saw as a basis for peace after the defeat of Germany, Austria-Hungary, and the Turkish Empire. Wilson eventually called for an independent Poland with access to the sea. Wilson's support for Polish independence proved to be crucial for the rebirth of Poland during the Versailles Peace Conference in 1919. Of course, these events increased interest in the United States in Poland and called for a second edition of Buszczyński's book. The author often remarked that Poland could learn from the American experience. He certainly emphasized the positive aspects of American history while ignoring many of the more negative realities.

Buszczyński visited the United States during the period historians refer to as the Progressive Era and he lauds President Theodore Roosevelt. He does not, however, mention the inequalities, problems, and social unrest of the period. While the author does mention some American faults, especially bribery, for Buszczyński the United States is a beacon of hope. Of course, this attitude must be seen from the perspective of the times. America had entered the Great War and helped to defeat the Central Powers. It was the greatest industrial power of the era and its reputation as a model of democracy seemed unrivaled.

Buszczyński showed interest in the Polish diaspora to the United States, noting that he had been told that Chicago's Polish and Czech populations are larger than either Warsaw's or Prague's (although this was not in fact the case). He recognizes Chicago as the largest settlement of Poles in the country and the tendency of Polish immigrants to live in urban areas. The author makes the statement that Poles in the United States were not prone to losing their nationality, but held on to it and exhibited a good deal of *polskość* or Polishness. Like other Polish visitors, he mentions the adulteration of the Polish language as it is spoken in the diaspora. This is a constant source of concern from Sienkiewicz in the 1870s to today. Buszczyński lauds the patriotism of Polish Americans and claims they could be an example for European Poles. He even states that the American Polonia would likely offer both blood and treasure for the cause of Polish independence. Of course, this proved true during World War One when Polish Americans raised an army to fight for Polish independence and sent millions of dollars to the homeland for war relief of the Polish population. The author also notes that Polish Americans joined together in fraternal organizations and raised large amounts of money to build monuments to Kościuszko and Pułaski, both heroes of the American Revolution. He bemoaned the fact that there was little interest in Poland about the diaspora.

Of course, the author also mentions the negative aspects of Polish-American culture. Buszczyński mentions disagreements, interparty warfare and slander and the fact that Poles are intolerant of each other. The author also noted the fact of alcoholism, juvenile delinquency, and crime. He refers to Polish immigrants as slovenly and less civilized. This betrays his social class background and prejudices. Of course, this attitude also reflects the perception of their status in the United States as members of poor working-class communities. At the time the majority of Polish immigrants labored as unskilled workers in slaughterhouses, steel mills, coal mines, and other industries. Buszczyński was an upper-class landowner in Poland and an entrepreneur. He was highly educated and well connected politically and socially in Kraków. His life experience was vastly different from the typical Polish immigrant to the United States. It is not surprising that he did not explore the roots of Polonia's poverty and social problems. This was not his aim in writing *Impressions of America*. In Chicago and other American cities, Polish Americans settled in the most crowded residential areas. Child death rates were high and the realities of poverty were everywhere. Buszczyński felt that American society had an edifying impact on individuals and mentioned several Polish immigrants whose lives had changed as a result of living in the United States.

This short book is a look at the impression the United States made on a Polish intellectual and entrepreneur before World War One. While it may paint too rosy a picture of America, it also should be seen as an introduction of the American experience to a Poland on the verge of a national rebirth. Buszczyński saw America as a successful optimistic counterweight to a Europe that had been enmeshed in a suicidal struggle during World War One. For many Poles the United States seemed a bright beacon of democracy and a model for Poland, in particular, as it emerged from 123 years of partition. The United States was a large, diverse, and prosperous land that Buszczyński and others hoped would provide a model for the Second Polish Republic.

Dominic A. Pacyga, Ph.D.
Chicago, Illinois

Stefan Buszczyński's Tenets as Recorded in his Literary Testament

Only light and virtue will redeem nations, and hence society, and so lead humankind onto the path illuminated by natural laws.

There is no equality between people other than the one that brings them closer together, or makes them equals, with the aid of light and virtue.

Within the social system the only statutory rights, the only privileges, and the only ranks available to individuals should be those that are shaped by education and virtue.

Each person's sphere of activity should be marked out by their level of cultivation and their moral rectitude.

In practice the whole social system is determined by its electoral system. If the electoral system is good, the structure of society is sound; if the electoral system is flawed, the workings of society will be flawed.

Universal suffrage without regard to an individual's level of education and morality is a catastrophe for society.

Hence the electoral system should be based entirely on laws whose span is marked out using levels of cultivation and moral rectitude evidenced as the units of measure.

The rights of an individual, hence the rights of families, and hence the rights of nations are binding on society in its entirety.[1]

Preface to the Second Edition

A lively public interest in the United States has induced me to publish a second edition of my *Impressions of America* — the impressions I first formed several years before the Great War started in Europe. The stand taken by Americans in the current upheaval in the world order has reinforced the high esteem in which I hold this nation.

In the cataclysm of the European War, when humankind was in dire need of such a man, a providential statesman did emerge. It was not a military general as expected, but a man who was an American university professor and the President of the United States. In his speeches he gave voice to American public opinion and in the first of his addresses about peace, on 28th January 1917, he proposed essential principles that should be followed to bring justice and freedom back to the world. When his call was met by derision from the Germans, who were intoxicated by bloodletting, looting and self-worship, when the future of the unhindered development of the United States was threatened, this committed pacifist did not hesitate to reach for arms to defend humankind's loftiest ideals. That was the will of the American nation. It understood that when confronted with evil intent, the use of force was necessary. The Americans knew that, if it occurred, a victory by the Central Powers would amount to world conquest by the Prussian menace and a triumph for the ancient principles of Caesarism — incompatible with the foundations on which the New World had based its development. Disturbing these foundations would, sooner or later, make it impossible to maintain the existing socio-political system in America — a system which, along with freedom, is valued by Americans above all else. In making this grave decision to go to war the Americans showed their usual fervour, treating the war as a crusade against the supremacy of "Might over Right" and a battle in defence of world freedom. They wished to put an end to wars waged by those who ruled by terror, incited nations to pillage and plunder, poisoned whole generations with false ideology for the sake of expanding their artificially created state structures, and rode roughshod over the views held by individuals and nations.

Wilson, voicing the nation's sentiments, put forward propositions that the governed had moral rights, the world order should follow the principle of national self-determination and that a league of nations should be established. Was this really a revelation of new, heretofore unknown truths to the world? Far from it, they were already embedded in the soul of every honest and right-thinking person; these were truths as simple as any straightforward truth. Yet, Europe, in its morass of moral barbarity, held the view that, although these principles might be just, for the time being they were impracticable and so it must persist with its old errors and transgressions; in contrast the American nation, with its dogmatic approach, its skill in directly putting its principles into practice, and its innate energy and boldness, stepped forward to fight for its guiding principles.

With the miseries of war evident for all to see, these principles quickly gained wider and wider acceptance, attracting hearts and minds and eventually triumphing over brute force, because they were moral. The mighty American nation stood ready to uphold these principles and the nation's spokesperson achieved a prominence never seen before in the history of nations: he dictated the terms of peace to the world.

Even the Germans, heretofore possessed by vanity and egotism, have started to turn over a new leaf by acknowledging President Wilson's plan for a new world order and deferring to it in all matters. Their pagan beliefs have been vanquished and they realise that a Christian civilisation's principles do not allow it to treat them in the way they would have treated the defeated side, had they been victorious. All the more is excessive pride humbled; all the greater is truth's triumph. Now they have been defeated both on the battlefield and in the moral sphere, the Germans may well have a change of heart and their idealism of old might be reawakened. Combined with their positive attributes it could once more make them a nation with lofty moral values, as they previously were until 1870. That was when they became inebriated with their own success in battle and Bismarck and all that German materialistic (hence pagan) philosophy contaminated and corrupted the whole of the current generation. In defeat Germany will once more take its place in the civilised world.

For thousands of years various rulers, conquerors and statesmen have striven to solve the problem of how to organise the societal system of the world. Some wanted to reach a solution through a universal monarchy, others through hegemony of the most powerful state, yet others by a system imposed at a congress or perhaps a system based on political equilibrium; all of these failed and engendered nothing but wars, misfortune and servitude. The basis on which solutions were sought was bogus; it violated natural laws as it overlooked the existence of national communities and was driven by personal interest and vanity. The solution was simple: national self-determination. This straightforward solution is in keeping with the natural order and Christian principles and it was put forward by America.

There are those who cannot comprehend and do not believe that America could have entered the war for the purpose of defending its guiding principles. Servitude, the desire for gratification and gross materialism have so debased European society that it can no longer comprehend a heroic stance or fighting for anything other than material gain. Due to its struggles for independence and also its earlier history, the Polish nation can well relate to the idea of making sacrifices and fighting for the sake of certain moral values, for truth and for freedom — their own freedom and the freedom of other nations. History has many examples of wars waged to uphold ideals. One only needs to mention the crusades and religious wars, Islamic wars, the expedition to Vienna to rescue Christendom, the war between the northern and southern States over the abolition of slavery and the many wars fought for nationalist causes. But even misguided ideals, or frankly evil ones, have inspired men to fight. If national aspirations and religious causes can lead men to wage war, what is so strange about the youthful and vigorous American nation being inclined to go to battle to defend aspirations relating to all humankind which coincided with their own aspirations?

The Swiss journalist E. Fueter, who is currently staying in America, emphasises the extremely idealistic nature of the Americans' motivation for participating in the war. He claims that apart from defending their democratic system, the main reason that the Americans went to war was an almost religious conviction that they ought to be advocates for justice and freedom in the world.

America achieved victory, but could not complete its mission as, after the preponderance of authority in Europe, anarchism reared its head, destroying all the foundations of civilised life and discarding all moral rules. It unleashed a wild rampage of the enslaved seeking in their turn to oppress others, seeking gratification, and seeking to make others suffer; they saw all aspects of civilisation as obstructions and all laws as restrictions on their "freedom", which in their view equated to being "free" to do anything they pleased. Lack of education, coarse manners and base instincts are now a passport to full citizenship, while pandering to these — is a passport to power. Will the populace, corrupted by the previous system and bestialised by war, manage to imbibe America's principles for life as a healthy community? We can see the abundance of suffering resulting from evil, but no sign of an abundance of virtue that could redeem Europe.

Perhaps an unexpected miracle will rescue it from further decline.

Poles in particular could learn a great deal from Americans. Many years of subjugation have developed in us a contempt for laws, an inability to organise and govern ourselves, distrust and resentment, and, in the end, fractiousness. Americans possess characteristics that are quite the reverse: an understanding of the need for laws and respect for them, an extraordinary aptitude for organisation and self-government, a sense of their own strength, composure in their dealings with others and an ease in finding agreement with other people. Closer ties with a society that possesses the virtues we lack might encourage us to acquire those virtues. To some extent this can be seen in the Polish community in America, whose members are, I believe, on average more worthy than the Polish populace in "the old country". Developing ties may be made easier due to certain core qualities being common to both the Polish and American character, namely: a strongly individualistic approach, a love of freedom, deep religious sentiment, and democratic beliefs. The cornerstones of the political system in the United States correspond to those of the previous system in Poland: power stems from the people, election of rulers, federation and a militia. Our republicanism was so strong that the monarchy was forced into wide-ranging modifications to conform to it. It was love of freedom and of human dignity that attracted Kościuszko to fight for America and made him hold America dear, as prof. Sobieski has demonstrated. Perhaps not all people who have come to know America have fallen in love with her, but all of them do feel respect. This feeling of respect developed during the current war, even in people who had not previously felt it because they did not know Americans and so had held a very sceptical view of their qualities. Establishing cultural and economic ties with America is currently one of the more important tasks faced by Poland.

Impressions of America

The first time I arrived in the United States, I came with preconceptions about America which were widely held back home. After a while I began to notice that my notions did not correspond to reality. I continued observing and became convinced that the reality was quite the opposite. The discrepancy between these viewpoints led others to persuade me to publish in print the observations I had articulated in letters to my family. I was encouraged to publish my insights by the fact that people who knew America without exception agreed with my views on American society, whereas differing convictions were expressed by those who had never visited.

Perhaps these passages will contribute to a more profound interest in this genuinely new world which differs so much from our own.

* * *

America! I am in America, the country that over the last 400 years has attracted millions of people who felt cramped and stifled in Europe; I am in that promised land, the land of freedom, where development of both the individual and society is natural and unhindered. An extraordinarily beautiful, rich, extremely dynamic country, a place where a man's energy can find an outlet and resources worthy of it, a place where he can find happiness and has in fact found it, and has been able to live in a way befitting a man but also following God's will.

On first coming face-to-face with America one is struck above all by a significant difference in people's countenances; these are people at ease, full of dignity, strength and the joy of life. When a certain high-ranking official from a European country's embassy asked what had struck me most about America I described my first impressions in the manner stated above. This diplomat, who understood Americans well, confirmed the accuracy of my observations saying, 'That's right. Here you do not see the pained, wretched faces seen so often in Europe. Here they feel the joy of life!'

Amongst the thousands of faces observed by my travelling companion Mr Fr. Pułaski and myself over several days in New York we noticed only a few that were dejected. Here you do not find that downtrodden, mistreated class of people so common in Europe, people without any hope for the future, fearful people chasing cheap gratification, without any strength, without any courage, without any self-confidence or gaiety. Here being exhausted and worn out by life is unknown.

Americans are jolly and sociable; their hearty manner doesn't offend as there is no arrogance in it, just self-confidence combined with considerable personal dignity. When an American stretches out his hand with his head held high one feels the power and candour in his handshake, his gaze is bright, composed and frank.

Americans are exceedingly easy-going and approachable. They are also trusting because they hold falsehood (other than in the form of exaggeration) in the greatest contempt. Making a statement suffices in place of providing proof, but woe betide the person who makes an untrue statement.

Mr R., a merchant from Prague in Bohemia, told me about an experience he found surprising: on deciding to spend a little while in America he had given instructions for his clothes to be sent over from Europe and when collecting them from the customs office he had made a declaration that they were his own previously worn clothes; he was allowed to take them free of any duty without the trunk being examined. 'How can you be sure that these are really used clothes?' said Mr R. 'Anyone could make a declaration like that!' 'You have made a statement, Sir,' replied the officer, 'there would be serious consequences for you if it were otherwise.'

I myself experienced exemplary treatment at the customs office when, due to certain formalities not having been observed, I had some difficulties in collecting a European shipment which contained a large number of copies of a sugar production map I had published. My declaration that this publication was not for sale was sufficient to secure exemption from customs duties. When I mentioned I was sorry to cause them so much trouble, they replied, 'No trouble, it's our job to make it easier for you to settle your affairs.'

It takes surprisingly little time for a newcomer to become conversant with American institutions, as they are intended to serve the needs of the public and those needs are accurately and logically anticipated.

One does not see people rushing around in agitation or at the end of their tether, one does not see people becoming irritated or quarrelling. Although Americans are very exuberant one is struck by their patience. At a hotel in New York

I watched as a certain inept cloakroom attendant struggled to supply a couple of gentlemen with their garments. They waited calmly, making the odd, good-natured joke about the attendant's ineptitude.

Newcomers from Europe are astounded by the unexpected courtesy, helpfulness and kindness of Americans. When someone turns to them for assistance they show a keen interest in the matter at hand. If they cannot provide an explanation themselves they will point you to someone else. Regardless of whether it is a passenger on a train, a clerk in a business, the head of a huge corporation, a high-ranking government official or a chance acquaintance, they will spare no effort to help a person asking for assistance. One might think it was just courtesy to an independent foreign tourist who has no need of any onerous services; however I soon became convinced that they were equally obliging when I turned to them in commercial matters.

The decent, kindly approach characteristic of Americans is revealed even more clearly by their attitude towards people in real need. Mrs B. related the following episode of her life as evidence of the great mercy and true neighbourly love which are characteristic and common traits among Americans. She came to America as a child with her little brother and her mother after the uprising in 1863, fleeing from Lithuania and Muravyov's persecution. Their financial reserves were quickly exhausted; her mother worked in a cigar factory for several years to provide for her family, but in time fell seriously ill. The neighbours supported the sick woman and her children and a job was found for the girl at the factory where her mother had previously worked. Nevertheless the family was still in want.

One day the grocer called the young girl over and asked why she had stopped getting goods from his shop. 'We don't have the money to pay you for the goods we've already taken, let alone any more,' answered the girl. 'Well, that's understandable,' said the grocer, 'because your mother's ill, and that's good reason for you to need credit now. Make sure you come every day, as you did before, and get the essentials you need. You'll pay when you're in a position to do so.' A few months later the mother and children moved to another town. The shopkeeper, to whom they still owed money, facilitated their departure and threw in some supplies to get them through the initial phase of settling down in a new town.

Mrs B.'s daughter married and moved to Montrose, a small town in the Rocky Mountains, with her husband. The local men promptly helped the newcomer to enclose and plant a field and to repair the house; the female neighbours assisted the newly-wed woman with domestic duties for several weeks. Newcomers to any settlement are generally seen as new companions and welcomed.

Mr M. told me the story of how, when he found himself in a hopeless situation after arriving in America, a couple of Americans who heard about his plight raised him out of poverty, acted as guarantors and helped him to start a new life.

Mrs A., a good friend of mine, a highly intelligent person familiar with almost all of Europe, moved to Boston. She also expressed great admiration for American society. In order for her children not to lose contact with Poland she took them on trips back to their fatherland every few years, but even so she made the following point: 'I thank God above all that I have been able to bring up my children in the healthy and elevated atmosphere that exists here.'

I have been able to commence a business relationship with America thanks to the encouragement and endless helpfulness of people from the pertinent industrial and business circles. Both staff and the heads of huge companies acted as if it mattered to them to ease that journey for me. The Department of Agriculture provided me with a great deal of in-depth advice, indeed the Secretary of Agriculture himself learned that I was collecting essential data relating to seed development and production and invited me to pay him a visit during which he declared his readiness to conduct a whole series of trials in line with my directions. He added jokingly that, if necessary, I could turn to him and he would gladly assist me as he had 'a certain degree of influence' in the aforementioned Department. (He had already been the Secretary of Agriculture for over a dozen years!)

* * *

One of the very typical characteristics of Americans is whole-hearted patriotism which manifests itself at every opportunity due to their youthful enthusiasm. Since American patriotism is proud but not in the least aggressive it is entirely compatible with expressing patriotism for one's home nation, even for a nation with emotions as intense as those of the Poles. Americans relate to other nations as "kinsfolk": hence they say 'your German cousin', 'your French cousin', even 'your Arabian' or 'your Indian cousin'. It gives cause for thought that nations which in Europe show hostility towards each other and engage in fierce battles live peacefully and amicably alongside each other in the United States.

I believe the American way of resolving social issues shows a quality of brilliant simplicity. They like to quote dogmatic axioms which might come across as naivety or platitudes if the words were not in fact accompanied by genuine feeling and directly followed by attempts to implement these maxims. Hence the principles proclaimed by their statesmen through history are repeated, live on and have become accepted as commandments in their society. The most venerated of all is Washington, a genuinely great and mighty figure who is a credit to humanity. Due to his probity his principles have become dogmas in public and political life. Americans are conscious of Washington's nobility, of his moral worth. Independence was gained thanks to his strength of character.

A highly developed sense of personal dignity, ambition to achieve something, to become famous for something, to surpass others — these are the most distinctive traits of an American. He has no wish to bring others low, but he wants to stand higher himself. Defeated — he does not curse or become emotional; he considers it a necessary stage in his battle; outdistanced — he does not become discouraged, he gathers his strength and prepares to do battle afresh. If he achieves a personal best he is happy, but wants to progress. He feels a burning desire to work and to act. These traits are the root of the naive bragging and youthful superlatives about his own State, his own town and his own neighbourhood. Americans are not envious; they understand that a business expanding in their neighbourhood will enhance the value of their own property. They also make an effort to stimulate cultural activity in their locality and attract people who might do well for themselves there. Indeed a consortium in Los

Angeles which owned about 20,000 acres of land in California offered me 1,000 acres free of charge, on condition that I set up a research facility and seed production plant there. Such an enterprise would have stimulated other businesses, it would have been an advertisement for the area that a European who had travelled across the whole of the United States to develop a new branch of agricultural production had found that particular location was most suitable; it would have generated economic activity in the area, and the rest of their estates would have risen in price and found eager buyers. Unfortunately, I could not accept this offer as the location did not suit my aims.

The supposition that the dollar is all that matters to Americans and that they worship it is entirely erroneous; the cult of the golden calf stands on a much higher pedestal in Europe. Money is seen as a very valuable means to an end, but not as the goal. Hence, an American regards losing his fortune as a disagreeable episode in his life, but he is not disheartened or broken by it. He will work to build up his wealth once more.

It is much frowned upon if a person who has made their fortune does not allocate some of it to good causes during their lifetime or, at the very least, in a bequest. Hence the endowments for universities, schools, hospitals, public libraries etc. originate mainly from gifts and bequests, not infrequently sums of several million or even tens of millions of dollars.

It is not a matter of indifference how a person made their fortune or how they use their wealth. A certain rich man who was generally disobliging and had made his money by harming others offered huge sums of money for social and benevolent causes in order to clean up his reputation. His application to Congress for approval of his endowment trust was turned down, as was his offer to various societies.

Dr F. from Buffalo, our countryman, was a highly-rated physician and earned an annual income of about $15,000 from his practice. He was offered the position of chief medical officer for the municipality at a yearly salary of $4,000. Despite his total income reducing by half as a result he did not hesitate to accept the position. He gave these reasons: the total of his income streams although lower was sufficient for a comfortable life and to bring up his children; he felt gratified, especially as a Pole, to be the chief medical officer of a city with a population of half a million and to be able to accomplish something good for the general public, in particular for the Polish district.

* * *

Great and widely spread prosperity is evident all over America. Poverty appears only temporarily during economic crises and does so mostly in big cities. However when there is a shortage of jobs in the cities there is a labour shortage in the countryside. Poverty is more commonly seen in New York where almost two thousand emigrants arrive every day. Anyone who is able and wants to work will not experience poverty. Superbly organised public charity and compassion along with a willingness to help — not sentimental, but manly and strong — forestall destitution due to unfortunate circumstances.

Americans envisage philanthropy in the way expressed by Roosevelt, 'Anything that encourages pauperism, anything that relaxes the manly fiber and lowers self-respect, is an unmixed evil. In charity the one thing always to be remembered is that, while any man may slip and should at once be helped to rise to his feet, yet no man can be carried.'[2]

People imagine Americans work to the point of exhaustion in the pursuit of money, gasping for breath like a fast but short-winded horse. Not in the least! They concentrate on their work, stick to it, follow their plans, but above all they work skilfully. They put an enormous amount of energy into their work, they want to work and can do so continuously and in that sense it is a "strenuous life"[3], but in it there is no chaotic, fevered struggle, which either wears a man out or sucks him in and constricts him. Their habits and day-to-day lifestyle fit into a regular routine in terms of set times for working, eating, rest and play. Once the jobs are finished they go to the theatre, the circus, clubs and restaurants which are full of people relaxing and enjoying themselves. In all this that sociable, often hearty, unconstrained manner prevails, but it has no space for nasty thoughts; you can sense the innate good manners, deep-seated decency and propriety that lie behind it. Americans do not work longer than 8 hours. At 5pm, or 6pm at the latest, the offices close and even the warehouses shut down; by 7pm or 8pm — the streets are empty! The workers have dispersed to their homes — a large number of these are in the suburbs; the roads run on into the fields and woods where thousands of "diminutive manor houses" stand in small gardens. Such a detached house might cost 4 – 6 thousand dollars and be situated 10 – 20 km away from the central districts, but every few minutes there is a tram, elevated railway train or under-ground train running and one can get to the city centre for 5 cents (25 heller).

Prices in America are generally much higher than in Europe (I am referring to comparisons in 1910 and 1912), in other words the money is worth less. The exchange rate for the dollar is 5 krone, but in transactions the dollar is worth the same as the gulden is at home. However, relatively speaking life is not that expensive. Modest but adequate board and lodging costs about $30 a month. Earnings are significantly higher than in Europe. An unskilled labourer earns about $2 a day. The differential in remuneration between physical and mental labour is not as great as it is in Europe. An intelligent worker who does not hold a position of responsibility or one requiring special talents receives about $100 a month.

The law forbids attachment of the earnings of a person with a family when those earnings are less than 12 dollars a week.

Towns really do "grow" at lightning speed in America and extremely quickly take on the character of a larger, more cultured agglomeration of people. In this way Chicago, for example, whose settlements were built in 1830, is now one of the largest cities in the world with a population of over 2 million. The famous "skyscrapers" i.e. buildings with 15 or 20 floors and tower blocks with 40 – 50 floors are only intended to accommodate offices, stores and warehouses; the local people mainly live in villas and small houses occupied by single families. This explains the extraordinarily large space occupied by cities over there.

Parks and the sections in them set aside for children to play are particularly valued and well-tended. In the poor districts of the great cities houses are being either demolished or transported elsewhere intact in a sufficient number to make space for the creation of parks for children; in these parks small children have paddling pools and gravel to play with while the older children have playing fields, gymnastics apparatus, swimming pools etc. Americans have endless ideas about how to make spending time in the fresh air (called "out-of-door-life") more enjoyable for young people: it is something they treat as a matter of the utmost importance, just as the English do, for reasons of physical and moral hygiene. Within the parks there are usually reading rooms, meeting rooms and even small rooms with kitchenettes which can be hired for a nominal fee for the use of smaller private associations. It has been noted that following the establishment of such parks in neglected districts the number of criminals has greatly reduced. Americans' great love of nature has resulted in a custom whereby in the summertime a great many families go away to the mountains or prairies for a few weeks, often taking a tent or a wagon, to lead a nomadic life in nature's bosom (this is called "camping"). It is absolutely safe and weapons are superfluous.

* * *

Niagara! A beautiful evening in May, a wooded park full of charming greenery. A mighty roar can be heard in the distance, then a crash, a thud and drawn-out, distant thunder. A mighty, crazed torrent rushing forwards in a frenzy thrashes about ferociously, topples over rocks, breaks up over boulders, yielding to them in fury; it battles on in a thousand cascades, it pants foaming in desperate exertion yet rushes single-mindedly ahead, raging, fearsome and at the same time fearful. All of a sudden: a moment's concentration, contemplation, calm and then, as invincible as destiny, with the majesty of death, it plunges into the abyss, mighty, great and proud. It disappears in a haze, in silvery flurries, enveloped in mists and plumes, behind the mysterious curtain of iridescent shapes. This is just one branch of Niagara. A little further away huge billows of spray rise into the air and form amazing images. There a huge and mighty river fights, heaves and tosses in the same way; it also abruptly halts its flow, hesitates and then drops into the chasm. An elemental, uncurbed force grips the waves, sucks them in, yet they, imperturbably calm, resolute, valiant in the face of looming death, of a mysterious abyss, proceed in the midst of a raging battle to some new world, to a new form of existence; they transform into mist, into vapour, silvery billows, into fantastical jets, sometimes shooting into the air, sometimes desiring to return to their previous existence, sometimes obscuring all the dread of their internal tragedy which no human eye will ever see. One senses that an almighty battle is raging in this chaos, that great powers are grappling with each other, that cyclopean toil must be forging new forms of existence out of the chaos. And behold from this nebula, with all the momentum of new life, mighty waves swell up, join, and merge so that a massive, powerful, surge of water reborn from multiple sources once more flows majestically towards the sea.

I went behind the waterfall in the Cave of the Winds. Here the river has toppled over into a fit of frenzy. Sucking air into its mad rush, coalescing with it, in a mad whirl the river seethes, strikes, whips back and shoots into the sky. With relentless force a huge wave hits from above like a cyclopean hammer; it shatters against the rocks, it rises into the sky in columns of vapour, in terror it throws deranged drops like hailstones backwards at the rocky wall, which rebuffs this onslaught, this relentless storming by a whirlwind of torrents and watery missiles; the rock recedes terrified by the violence of the assault, astonished at the persistence of the attack, it recedes slowly but continually; already there is an enormous hollow carved into its side, so that the waves wail furiously, accompanied by the wind, and the light dies in the watery depths. The elements are fully engaged in this cataclysm and nature holds back terrified by this wrestling bout. Chaos and nothing but unbridled torrents, enraged winds, rocks, which will soon join in the dizzying whirl, the mad dance. The accompanying music is powerful, worthy of the participants — from thunderous thuds and artillery explosions to the plaintive keening of the autumn wind. Terrified mists push their way out of this menacing cave in a frantic panic. From above fresh battle units descend with unstoppable force one after the other: cold, menacing, they gather in formation, they boost their flow, they hurtle on and strike in one last mad charge. The ranks shatter, so one by one, in their endless multitude, they throw themselves into the deadly throes of the final battle. They will prevail!

* * *

Here is yet another of the numerous examples of the innate courtesy of the American people. Yesterday there was no admission to the Cave of the Winds as the funeral of the Superintendent of Niagara State Reservation (i.e. the area around the waterfall owned by N.Y. State) was taking place. The office staff, the attendants and the guides had gone to the funeral. A young boy was left behind to inform any tourists that a more senior member of staff would turn up by five o'clock. I waited until he arrived and explained that I had stayed that day in order to visit the cave and go down beneath the waterfall. I asked him to make an exception and let me visit that day, declaring my readiness to pay significantly more than the standard fee.

'The payment is not the issue,' he said, 'I would gladly help you, but it's not possible today as the guides have dispersed. What time do you leave tomorrow?'

'At eight twenty-five,' I replied.

'OK. We normally open at eight, but if you would like I could come earlier with some guides.'

'Seven o'clock then.'

'All right.'

The following day at five to seven he arrived at the entrance as I approached a few hundred paces behind him. He would not hear of any payment. I wanted to give $5 to charity to show my gratitude for his trouble and courtesy, it was the least I could do; however since there was no "collection" there he advised me to make my donation in the city.

* * *

Agriculture, trade and industry developed exceptionally well around the Great Lakes. Ease of transport by water, fertile soil, a humid but moderate climate and rich seams of coal provided favourable conditions. Recently part of Niagara Falls has been used to generate electricity, supplying 500,000 British horse-power worth of light and energy within a radius of several hundred kilometres.

There is more ship traffic in the harbours on the Great Lakes than in the great sea ports, particularly on Lake Michigan. To give an idea of the extent of these lakes, consider that for example the surface area of Lake Michigan (third in terms of size) is almost as large as the whole of Galicia.

Chicago, which lies on the shores of this lake, had 100 (explicitly: one hundred) inhabitants in 1831 but now covers an area more than 30 km long and about 20 km wide with a population of over two million people of many different nationalities; it is the fourth largest city in the world in terms of population. It is said there are more Poles in this city than in Warsaw and more Czechs than in Prague. Chicago is not only a city of trade and industry; it is also a centre of intellectual life.

Following contact with Polish communities in America and Poles dispersed individually or in small groups over a wide area of the United States, I have come to the conclusion that Poles are not prone to losing their national identity and very few do so. I saw children from the third generation to live in America who felt so intensely Polish they could serve as a model to our children, even though their parents had never been to Poland, even though their grandfather had emigrated from Europe at a young age. I saw numerous astonishing examples where the depth of patriotic feelings, cherished like the most precious treasure, quite simply tugged at my heartstrings.

National consciousness is awakening amongst the uneducated masses coming from Poland to the United States. Alongside all their American patriotism, Poles permanently resident in America care passionately about Polish national aspirations and try to preserve their traditions and keep their national identity. They are pained by the shortcomings in their own efforts, by their own lack of knowledge about their home country, their insufficient familiarity with its history and their adulteration of their native tongue. My impression, on the whole, is that patriotic spirit amongst Poles in America is on average at a higher level than in Poland itself. I also believe

Poles from America might be even more ready to sacrifice life and property for the Polish cause than Poles living in their own country. These phenomena can be explained by a higher level of culture and greater freedom in public life, by the influence of Americans' enthusiastic temperament and lastly by the undoubted remoteness of their ideal of Poland which is clouded by their yearnings.

Poles in America take a lively interest in what is happening in "the old country", but they do not have the opportunity to satisfy it due to the lack of contact with Poland. They are rightfully aggrieved that their brethren on the other side of the ocean do not — as indeed we do not — show much concern for them. 'We do not need material assistance from you, indeed that is something we may give to you, but we do need moral support, we need you to take an interest in our lives, maintain relations and exert influence via newspapers, associations and institutions. We would like your scholars and community organisers to visit us — we can cover the costs — and enlighten us about how you live, to get to know us and to teach us what we should do to serve Poland together. We are a large and strong community here, living mainly in close-knit groups, but we lack contact with our home country. We lack spiritual leaders, as those you send over from the intelligentsia generally have a negative moral influence. You send us the rejects, give us men.'

I encountered these opinions repeatedly, hearing them both from people with high social standing and from artisans and small-scale merchants etc.

When a sizeable deputation of American Poles visited Kraków in 1910, its members complained that no-one engaged with them. No-one engaged with people who had saved for a long period to cover the costs of the pilgrimage and had travelled to Poland with hearts quickening in anticipation: they were not given the opportunity to express their opinions, to develop closer ties or to garner any knowledge or spiritual nourishment. This was indeed the case.

Following prevailing customs and to satisfy their needs, Poles in America readily group together to form associations, many of which have enormous numbers of members and substantial funds at their disposal. The latter are mainly associations of associations. As a consequence "parliaments" consisting of delegates from each individual member association are established. Their resolutions have executive force since these associations, even those formed for general purposes, are set up as mutual assurance societies: if one of the member associations fails to apply the resolutions passed by the "parliament" it can be excluded and would lose the privileges acquired by prior contributions. The member association is responsible to the central board and it in turn can force its own members to apply the resolutions by threatening exclusion and loss of contributions. In this way an assembly was able to pass, for example, a resolution regarding a few cents' levy to fund the monument to Kościuszko in Washington. Naturally there were those who opposed this but nonetheless they had to pay, until tens of thousands of dollars had been amassed and a monument to the victor of the battles at Saratoga and Racławice was erected close to the White House. It was created by the sculptor Antoni Popiel from Lwów (may he rest in peace) and is one of the most beautiful monuments I have ever seen. Kościuszko is shown dressed in a United States officer's uniform gesturing with a battle plan of Saratoga. His expression conveys vigour and yearning. On the pedestal to one side, a dying Polish officer is held up by a scythe-bearing infantryman from Kraków, and charges him with the continuation of the battle and the future of the nation. On the other side an American officer uses a sabre to slice through the bonds of an American settler. To the sides: the European hemisphere and on it a snake, stretched out from Mongolia all the way to Poland, endeavours to bite the eagle rising up above the globe; the eagle is bristling in deadly battle with the snake; on the opposite face the American hemisphere on which the American eagle is calmly landing amongst laurels and olive branches. The monument bears the inscriptions 'Kościuszko', 'Saratoga', 'Racławice' and Campbell's verse, 'And freedom shrieked when Kościuszko fell.' The US government approved this monument and the official unveiling took place at the same time as the unveiling of the monument to Kazimierz Pułaski erected on the authority of a resolution by Congress.

Standing at the base of Kościuszko's memorial looking at the face of the pensive Polish peasant holding a scythe, a symbol of both labour and battle, curious thoughts crossed my mind, almost a vision, that our nation had to pass through America before it could return, reborn and strengthened, to rebuild Poland.

The names Kościuszko and Pułaski are highly respected by Americans and serve Poles to this day as a form of entitlement conferring the right to citizenship of the United States.

The fundamental reasons are without doubt the facts that a Polish national hero of the stature of Kościuszko fought for America's freedom before he led our nation, that after the fall of Poland once he was freed from prison Kościuszko returned to

America, and that there was a bond of friendship between him and both Washington and his successor President Jefferson. Professor W. Sobieski points out the analogy between the political systems in Poland and the United States and notes that Kościuszko was an ardent admirer and advocate of the ideas of the New World.

'Kościuszko,' says prof. Sobieski, 'personifies the fusion of Polish and American ideals. Not only did he stand on the ramparts of the old Polish-Lithuanian Commonwealth, but he also built fortifications to defend the new republic emerging beyond the Atlantic Ocean. This pre-eminent Polish emigrant brought new ideas from the other hemisphere back to his fatherland and tried to relate them to long-existing Polish ideas and to reinforce the latter, even when it was contrary to Europe's wishes.'[4]

'The role Lafayette played in the French Revolution as the champion of American ideas, such a role, indeed an even greater role, was played in Poland by Kościuszko. Subsequently, while Europe was absorbing many American ideas through France as an intermediary, Poland had already encountered these ideas both earlier and directly from America through Kościuszko.'[5]

Despite the change in circumstances the Polish national character still manages to exhibit itself in America: disagreements, interparty warfare and slander; empty boasting and fabrication by the ringleaders to cover up their moral deficiencies. Poles are intolerant of each other, yet they are submissive with non-Poles and unable to insist on their own rights. Looking at the population as a whole the cultural level of Polish society in America is higher than in Poland, yet one continually feels the lack of suitable, more highly developed social strata which can bestow character and direction, influencing both their own community and others. However the Poles' level of culture appears less high when compared to other nations. Particularly in their own districts Poles are careless, slovenly and there are many accidents and crimes. Drunkenness is relatively widespread which greatly offends Americans. Due to this cultural inferiority Poles are not seen as a desirable or valued immigrant element in America. They do value Poles more than Jews, who pretend to be Poles here, as they do back home, nevertheless Poles are placed somewhere at the very end of the list amongst Italians, the Irish, Russians etc. Polish emigrants are mainly concentrated in the cities and manufacturing or mining settlements. Poles are not eager to work on farms, not even those who are settling in America for good, even though this would be the most suitable type of occupation for the Polish masses. Acquiring land has been made very easy and a farmer who puts in the work on the land himself is left with not only a very handsome income of \$15 – \$25 per acre, that is 100 – 160 krone per morgen, but also a significant surplus in value. Mr Jan Smulski, one of the most distinguished Poles in America, believes farm settlement in concentrated groups should be a policy aim for our emigrants; he argues that by working the land the Polish worker could become his own master and achieve prosperity and social standing.

Nearly every Pole in America talks of returning to "the old country", but they mean they wish to return to a free Poland with a political system like the one they have sampled in America. In reality many return after a year, fewer and fewer return after two or three years and only a negligible number do so after five. The vast majority of returning emigrants go to

Galicia, very few go to the Russian Partition and almost no-one returns to the Prussian Partition.

Fr. W. Kruszka's work entitled *Historja Polska w Ameryce* published in 1905 in Milwaukee, Wis. provides many interesting facts about the Poles in America. According to this work up to 2 million Poles lived in the United States in 1900. That year 450,000 people moved permanently to the United States from Europe; the figure includes 33,000 Poles i.e. over 7%. Since 1905 the number of immigrants to the United States has been around a million each year. Even if the percentage of Polish immigrants has reduced then taking into account the growth in the local Polish population the number of Poles in the United States would be approaching 3 million. Poles mainly live in the States around the Great Lakes (Illinois, Wisconsin and Michigan) and in Pennsylvania, New York and Massachusetts. This source gives a figure of up to 240,000 Poles in Chicago alone in 1900.

On its own initiative the city council of Buffalo organised an exhibition about how people lived in the Polish district. Diagrams, statistics, photographs and specimens illustrated how hard-working and thrifty Poles were, but at the same time exposed a low level of culture, neglect, the existence of an inordinately large number of taverns, significant crime, and the low proportion of skilled workers and hence the relatively low pay and low-level occupations.

Since Poles, who lived in close proximity to each other, made up 25% of the overall population of Buffalo the municipal authorities understood that the development of the city depended to a significant extent on improving this less civilised mass of people and giving them the opportunity to earn a better living. Hence it was necessary to establish schools teaching vocational skills for crafts and industry in the Polish district, to open crèches and to increase the number of reading rooms and lecture halls. The city allocated $500 a month for the upkeep of the municipal library in the "Dom Polski" Polish community centre.

The key idea behind this policy was to better and improve the weaker and less able, rather than harassing and persecuting them.

A similar method is used with juvenile offenders who are often placed into the care of a family with whom they live. Evident improvement and good behaviour on the part of the juvenile offender leads to release; however in cases where the guardian declares to a judge that the family can no longer take responsibility for them, the young person will be detained in a young offenders' institution.

* * *

America's edifying influence is illustrated by the following example. In B. I became acquainted with the S. family. Mr & Mrs S. were both busy working for themselves and for the community; their house was kept modestly but comfortably and made an agreeable impression on me; their numerous children were being brought up well and in a Polish spirit. Mr & Mrs S. had lived in B. for a few years and were well respected, although there were mutterings about their surname not being quite right and their European past being murky. But in the United States people do not ask needless questions about what a person did back in Europe, instead they look at how that person acts in America! A global indulgence is granted for the past. However, Mr S. was standing as a candidate for a high-level honorary position in an association. In these circumstances his record needed to be checked. Enquiries were submitted to the police in Kraków and the response advised the man supposedly called Mr S. had a different name; he had been convicted for crimes of theft, fraud and burglary on a number of occasions in Warsaw, Łódź and Germany; and he had been handed over to the Russian authorities by the authorities in Kraków. He escaped from there to America with his family and adopted the surname S. When this was exposed his candidature fell through of course and he was answerable to the government of his State for making false statements upon settling in the United States. In an open letter Mr S. admitted to most of the criminal charges against him, but gave the following explanation, 'While I was living in the demoralising conditions prevailing in Poland under Russian rule I did indeed act like a scoundrel — but you know all about my life and work in the last 9 years since I settled among you in B. Have I not worked wholeheartedly and honestly? Is there anything you can fault in my life here?'

Many people did not in fact break off their previous relations with him.

Here is another example, less extreme, but also typical. Mr X., a landowner from Podolia who was a "nice fellow", but an idler, a spendthrift and a bit of a feather-brain, lost his fortune and left for America. There he got to work: he worked as a photographer, he carried beams in the port etc. A year later he went back to Poland where he told his story in a very frank and straightforward manner. He intended to return to America because, as he put it, 'I am a person who just wouldn't be able to work in the conditions prevailing here, but over there I can do all sorts of work.'

* * *

I am tearing into the very heart of the American continent at a speed of 40 – 50 miles[i] an hour. I fly past the rich, beautiful fields of Illinois, scattered with farms that look like smart villas. In a few hours I will cross the Mississippi, in the evening the Missouri, and then I will find myself in the great open spaces of Nebraska and Colorado. The countryside at first reminds me of Ukraine, and then the Kherson area. The forests have disappeared, the vegetation is becoming weaker and weaker, and ashen in hue. The desolate prairies are covered in short, fine but nutritious grass (called buffalograss) and a type of sage unsuitable for grazing (called sage-brush). Endless plains. A desert landscape. The train races on in a straight line for hours on end so that the eye gets lost in the bewildering vastness. From time to time there are gravelly knolls; in the midst of this lifeless landscape astonished prairie dogs (a type of rodent similar to our hamsters) stand up like little posts, staring at the monster that is rattling, roaring and tearing through their habitation. It is a desert land, a hopeless land... but not so for Americans! Life is awakening in this wilderness. Here and there a plough cuts into the earth, a windmill emerges drawing water from deep below, or a small farm appears, not yet shaded by its recently planted trees. Elsewhere a settlement is being established. There are few houses as yet, but the church and school are standing; they are building an electric tramway which cuts

---

i 1 English mile = 1.6 km.

through the prospective districts of the blueprint to enable them to come into existence in reality; they establish gardens and parks, arable fields with lush greenery and so a focal point for human life is coming into being. In a few years' time there will be a beautiful, wealthy town here, in a dozen or so it may have a hundred thousand inhabitants.

Where has this oasis suddenly sprung from? Nearby an irrigation canal has been constructed and from it channels run sideways and transform the barren land of the desert into fertile soil — and in this way Americans build their country.

The train pounds on into the distance for hours on end, it devours the expanses. Again the endless grey emptiness — lifeless and menacing.

Besides the lack of rainfall, the eradication of more luxuriant plant life has been assisted by prairie fires that used to be started by American Indians to make the grass grow better on the pastures, as well as accidental fires of dried-out grasses. Once fire took hold in one part of the prairie, a whole series of fires would follow downwind, ignited by people who saw the approaching smoke on the horizon. When escaping from the fire, these people would burn the prairie behind them before the conflagration reached it, and would later shelter in the burnt-out areas. One feels a measure of humiliation being whisked through these endless expanses in a comfortable railway carriage in view of the fact that preceding generations marked their onward march to the Far West through the same prairies with their bones. What induced them to venture deep into this wild terrain? It was an empty, waterless, terrifying place where fires and hurricanes, hunger and thirst, exertion and exhaustion allied themselves with the Red Indians who were continually lying in wait, attacking people and torching the prairies — anything to scare away the reckless travellers. They were drawn by the lure of a country as huge and uncharted as the sea, by a lust for adventure and by incredible tales about the marvels of the Far West. There at the limits of the prairies lay an earthly paradise: imposing mountains, refreshing rains, fertile valleys, many varieties of game in vast forests, rivers full of fish, gold deposits and miracles — the unseen miracles of nature. So for months on end these processions of "conquerors of the unknown" marched on. Anyone who moved away from their wagon train was doomed, but even quite large expeditions perished due to wild forces of nature or at the hands of even wilder Red Indians whose intuition told them the fiercely determined palefaces might become the masters of these lands. Palefaces perished, but in their place further processions marched on and opened new lands to civilisation.

The further west one goes the more desert-like the landscape. The air is so limpid that contours huge distances away are clear and sharp, but in spite of this the eye cannot detect anything on the horizon, which is covered by an unblemished azure sky. Suddenly, to the west, a long string of small white clouds appear just above the horizon. It is the Rocky Mountains! Somewhat less than two hundred miles still separates us. The train will continue for a long time yet to race along the desert plateau more than 5,000 feet above sea level. We are approaching Denver; at last there is water — invigorating water brought down from the mountains — and the life it brings forth. Denver is a large, extremely affluent city at the base of the mountains. It was established in 1858 and currently has a population of over 200,000; it is a focal point for the very significant mining, industrial and agricultural activity of the State of Colorado.

Near Denver, but actually in the Rocky Mountains, are the abundant gold mines at Cripple Creek. These mines were discovered by a trapper who had been searching for gold for years and almost died of hunger on a number of occasions. The route to the mines from Colorado Springs is stunningly beautiful. Colorado Springs is the centre of the mining company's business; next to the small but smart town an extensive villa district stretches along an unbelievably beautiful valley all the way to Mannitou; at Mannitou there are hot springs at the base of Pikes Peak (which is as high as Mont Blanc, but easily accessible). No alcohol is sold in the whole of this region. Years ago the previous owner of the land gave it to the local authorities as a gift, but imposed a restriction that alcohol should not be sold there. All the current plot holders have to respect this rule. In many townships, counties and even, to the best of my knowledge, in some States the populace has voluntarily passed resolutions prohibiting the sale of alcoholic beverages.

Colorado, previously an infertile region, now possesses valuable mines, many factories of various types, prosperous farms and a dozen or so sugar factories. The Arkansas River which flows through Colorado has been totally depleted for irrigation needs. All around it there is empty prairie with scanty vegetation, as is generally the case in Colorado in places the irrigation system does not reach; only the crickets sizzle under the burning skies.

Areas the water does not reach are used as pastureland: thousands of heads of cattle graze unattended there, driven out onto the prairies for the whole summer. It is dangerous to venture there on foot as the cattle only refrains from attacking riders. One also needs to be alert to the danger of the numerous rattlesnakes which nest in dry areas. As autumn approaches an expedition of cow-boys rides deep into the prairies and mountains, surrounds these pasturelands and rounds up the cattle. The owners then divide the cattle up between themselves on the basis of the marks branded onto their hides. The new offspring are allocated on the assumption that calves keep close to their mothers and the heads of cattle whose owners cannot be identified are allocated in proportion to the size of each person's holding of cattle out to fodder. Some of the cattle die over the summer, victims to the prairie-wolves (although not many of these have survived) or due to other mishaps; some go astray; sometimes they find themselves with extra heads of cattle not belonging to the locals. The major breeders' brands would generally be recognised and in those cases a message would be sent that their cattle had turned up. Theft of cattle from the pastures is an exceedingly rare occurrence. It would not be possible to sell any stolen cattle and if caught the thief would face the severe punishment meted out by locals who take the law into their own hands.

In Colorado I stopped somewhat longer in a typical small American town called Rocky Ford. It has a sugar factory and is famous for melon production (cantaloupes). The town has about 5,000 residents, a couple of secondary schools, a few primary schools, 6 churches, a public library, a lecture hall, a beautiful park which of course includes a playground i.e. a place where children can play... but not a single tavern. The sale of alcoholic beverages, including beer, is prohibited in the whole township. There are no hansom cabs, but there are about 90 privately owned automobiles. The town hasn't been cobbled, but the pavements are made of cement, serviceable and clean. A small sign displays the notice, 'Spitting on sidewalks prohibited. Penalty $5.' It reminds me of a similar warning I saw in a municipal railway carriage in New York, 'Spitting prohibited. Penalty $100 fine, 1 month imprisonment or both.' Short, to the point and effective. In this small town there is, as is the case in most American towns, an association whose aims are to improve the town in all respects. Members of this association wear a badge which says, 'How?' When at home it is supposed to remind them to consider how they might help improve their town and when travelling to take note of practices elsewhere that would be worth introducing at home.

In Rocky Ford I witnessed a street incident which I consider worth noting because prof. van Dyke, an expert on American attitudes, says, 'An American always takes the side of the under dog.'[6]

Two dogs started snapping at each other on the pavement. The Americans standing nearby, smoking their pipes, watched the fight without taking sides. In the end one dog seized the other by the throat and knocked it to the ground, but then wouldn't let go. That crossed the boundary of gentlemanly combat. The men tried to pull the winner off, but it had sunk its teeth so deep into its opponent that a walking stick did not suffice to prise its jaws apart. So they fetched a pail of water and tipped it over the dog, which then let go of the dog in its jaws, while one of the spectators scolded the winning dog for 'unfair stubbornness'.

* * *

Contrary to widely held notions, American farms are not latifundia. In fact there are very few large landed estates. The usual type of agricultural holding is a farm consisting of a complex which can be worked by one family assisted by some farmhands. A farmhand, the equivalent of our *fornal*, earns 40 – 50 dollars a month and gets full board and appropriate lodging. Farms are mostly between 80 and 160 acres in size (1 acre = 2/3 morgen). Kansas has properties, e.g. farms, of 320 acres each, which are regarded as large holdings. Significant areas of land are owned by various Companies, in particular railway companies, but these divide land up into plots and speculate with them. Generally extensive farming techniques are used without applying crop rotation principles, however there is substantial use of extremely practical agricultural tools with the aim of replacing expensive and scarce farm labour. A man working in the fields — women hardly ever work on the land — gets a daily wage of about $2, which can rise to up to $5 when there are urgent tasks to complete. However the labourers work so intensively that if one takes into account the amount of work completed, the costs are not much higher than ours. There are not many areas of land left which are unoccupied and ready for immediate cultivation, however there are significant areas of uncultivated land which would be suitable for agricultural production if they were cleared of trees or irrigated.

The fact that agriculture is developing just as well in central and western States, which have inadequate levels of rainfall, as it is in the east, where the rainfall levels match those in a Western European climate, gives cause for thought. Work, and only work, has created conditions favourable to the development of agricultural production in those areas. A farmer who is always blessed with good weather and can water his fields when he chooses is in a better position than the farmer who is dependent on the vagaries of the weather. Joint-stock Companies and Ventures are springing up to exploit for agricultural purposes a greater portion of the land in places where due to lack of rainfall only fine grasses had previously grown. These companies block off whole mountain valleys and create networks of channels to distribute water all over the territory they have purchased. Land which was previously of no use then gains in value and is sold off to individual farmers. Blocking off valleys with massive dams creates waterfalls which are utilised to generate electricity used for lighting and for powering agricultural machinery. Areas of land which are not suitable or have not yet been exploited for agriculture are used for pastureland: huge herds of cattle graze there overseen by a few cow-boys.

Cow-boys lead lives full of adventure with shades of the knight errant; they live at close quarters with nature and have a close bond with it, trying to deepen their understanding of it and its mysteries. This life builds up their boldness, agility, stamina and courage. They are generally liked despite being somewhat quarrelsome, but they never exceed acceptable limits as that would be beneath the dignity of a cow-boy.

All work is respected in America; it is hard to find a person who hasn't moved from one occupation to another in the course of their working life: a farmer or a servant one day, an industrialist or a journalist the next, and then later a lumberjack or a government minister. Specialisation taken to its utmost limits, turning human labour into a series of mechanical tasks, is rarely seen here. Simplicity and excellent working practices facilitate enterprise in highly populated districts. Those who have more energy and capital have plenty of scope for action in the less populated regions. In all types of businesses jobs are allocated so that initially a person is given positions which require physical labour. Doctor B. who has a university degree from Berne started off as a cow-boy when he came to America, then he was given a post stubbing hops for a sugar factory and only once he had done this job well and it became apparent that he knew his chemistry was he offered the task of setting up a laboratory. He continued to work as a general operative until the laboratory was ready. In the end he became the managing director of the factory. Mr W. who completed his higher education at an agricultural college in Bavaria and managed an estate in Hungary was given the job of mowing alfalfa on arrival in America, afterwards he was a field supervisor for a long period, and in the end he became the agricultural director of a very large business. Americans say that you can spot a smart and resilient person even while they are loading manure. Starting from physical labour and the more lowly occupations is actually a matter of policy in America. The purpose of it is for the worker to get to know the business in which he works in more detail, for the brightest to build up experience and better themselves, and finally to show that all types of work matter. A person with expectations of obtaining a higher-level post straight away on the basis of diplomas or recommendations will definitely not achieve their aim — they must start at the beginning!

European engineers are amazed at the simplicity of Americans' solutions to technical problems. This is particularly striking in railway structures. An American technician can achieve the same result using primitive means as his European counterpart using highly complicated apparatus. The inventions of Edison, Bell and Wright are good examples of this. In the field of plant breeding the brilliant Luther Burbank operates without the assistance of scientific biological investigations, instead he heads straight for his goal and achieves excellent practical results. The same ingenious simplicity that is applied in their solutions to social problems is also a feature of the American technician's way of thinking. It results from leaving the individual's ability to develop unfettered. There is no culture of imposing restrictive formalities on a person who wishes to study nor is there any obligation to climb a hierarchical ladder of preparatory studies, no need for permissions, qualifying in terms of age etc. Examinations set by the school and by life will show whether a particular individual knows how to derive benefit from their studies. It irritates European theoreticians that unlearned Americans often achieve results which Europeans have not managed to attain. America produces very few learned abstractionists. Generally in America people are treated as adults, as people free to act as they choose, responsible for themselves and their attitude to others; they are not cosseted nor coddled. Orders, prohibitions, rules and regulations are kept to a minimum.

* * *

The Europeans who came to America drove out the indigenous population in fierce battles, however it needs to be stated that the white settlers who found themselves far from organised society engaged in vicious battles with the American Indians as they pushed into wild and distant territories. The federal government and the governments of individual States have issued and still continue to issue a whole series of laws intended to protect American Indians from exploitation by the squatters. One of the forms this protection took was granting American Indians individual tenure of large allotments of land which they could freely choose within designated zones. However since the settlers often swindled American Indians out of their individually-owned property the government granted large reservations of land to whole tribes, to be held as jointly-owned property; it was not possible to alienate these lands. Apart from this the government constantly issues American Indians with allocations of wheat and clothing as a tribute payment to the beaten side; lastly it has granted them the privilege of travelling on the railways free of charge. In view of the immense damage alcohol was wreaking on the American Indians the federal government prohibited selling or giving away intoxicating liquor to Indians under penalty of severe punishment.

It seems odd that the privileged position of the Red Indians is contributing to their degeneration and decline. As they did not have any higher needs and as the need to fight for existence was missing once they were transferred to a condition of peaceful prosperity, these warlike peoples, which had previously engaged in continuous battle with nature and the enemies of their tribes, went into decline. On the vast expanses of America with their inordinate, concealed riches had lived a population of barely three million nomadic hunters, who needed huge areas of land to support their way of life. Along came the white race which could fit a population of hundreds of millions into the same area. It is self-evident that when these two cultures met the lesser one could not survive.

There are approximately 350,000 Red Indians in America. Government expenditure on them is approximately $18 million a year, that is about $260 per capita. Almost all the tribes have now become relatively civilised. Naturally, they have their own schools. The number deprived of liberty (from the Apache tribe) in 1912 was 261.

Although the American Indians are far from the romanticised characters commonly portrayed in stories — they were, and in the main still are, essentially savage — their great bravery, pride, love of freedom and defence of their own country have earned them the sincere respect of other Americans. "The noble Red" is a widely used epithet. Americans are proud to have a trace of Indian blood in their families, whereas family ties with Negroes are viewed with scorn. The slavery endured by the Negroes has left its shameful mark on them.

There has been a great clamour about the attitude of Americans towards Negroes. This race, which is indeed lower, is not held in high regard by Americans, but has the benefit of full citizens' rights. In the southern States separate compartments for "coloured" travellers do indeed exist. In the northern States Negroes generally work as servants, but they are treated with dignity. At public meetings I repeatedly saw Negresses sitting beside American ladies without offending anyone.

Attitudes to immigration by the Oriental races are a serious and difficult issue. The Chinese and Japanese, who are extremely hard-working and have unbelievably low expectations, constitute menacing competition to the white worker: they have a very significant depressing effect on the rates of pay and export their savings to their own country. The inflow into the United States of these alien groups, which of course never assimilate into their host country, was increasing at an alarming pace. In the end Congress passed a law prohibiting further immigration from China and Japan. This is one of the main reasons for the antagonism between the United States and Japan and may trigger serious conflict in the future. Japan is trying to widen its sphere of influence in Mexico as it can more easily keep the Union in check from there.

* * *

Americans are principled, honest and scrupulous in private life, just as they are in business. An 'All right' — is binding. 'Honesty is the best Policy'[7] is the American's motto.

Observing their lives and culture one sees what an enormous chasm separates us from them, how much higher the level of civilisation is than in Europe. In the practicalities of life an amazing harmony exists between the interests of society and those of the individual, or more strictly speaking between the interests of the state and its citizen. Nobody tries to stand up against public opinion or the directives of the authorities, whose power is absolute and harshly enforced to an extent not envisaged by anyone in Europe. The police have a great deal of power, but it is power used in the service of society, which wants to and does obey the laws it has itself passed. This is genuinely republican discipline and respect for the law. Demonstrations and marches are allowed, but only with the knowledge of the police and strictly as scheduled. Yesterday, i.e. the 30th April, the socialist 1st May celebration took place; yes, it was yesterday because today i.e. 1st May is a Sunday and all protests, marches and concerts are forbidden here on Sundays. Sundays are reserved for God alone!

During the commemoration a group of Russian socialists hung up a red flag and wanted to demonstrate in a way for which they had not obtained permission. They were asked to stop their protest; since they didn't agree to do so a few policemen arrived with truncheons and the demonstrators soon disappeared.

Despite (or perhaps as a result of) the democratic, freedom-loving political system of the United States, socialism does not flourish there. It is not subjected to harassment by means of the law. The pronounced individualism and love of freedom which run deep in an American's soul create a barrier to the spread of socialist doctrine. People who come to America as socialists usually change their views.

The difference between the moral maturity of American society and our own ill-fated society is very great; in our society overblown individualism laid the groundwork for the proliferation of harmful elements as we embraced negation from the Germans, nihilism from the Russians and from the Jews — destabilising principles that act on the both the soul of the individual and the soul of society in a highly destructive manner. So in instances where, in Russia for example, the individual is restricted, here the individual is free. In instances where over there the individual is able to act according to their own idiosyncratic point of view even though it violates laws and customs, here they willingly accept not just the written laws, the statutes, but also the common law which actually guarantees the individual substantial freedom.

The public abides by the law and observes customary norms on its own: individuals are prepared to back up these rules with their own personal validation. The most extreme expression of this is the lynch which is carried out in clear-cut cases of shocking and serious criminality.

Freedom entails not hindering people from doing right, but by no means tolerating "I'll do as I please" behaviour. Moral principles play a decisive role here; the individual is responsible for their actions to society as a whole. Individuals are wholesome, happy and strong here because they acknowledge moral rules and comply with them; they exhibit skilful self-restraint; and they bring order, harmony and regulation to both the sphere of moral concepts and to material reality. Here there is no anarchy in the soul nor decadent relish of debasement; they do not abjectly bemoan evil and misfortune; there is no scepticism and they do not fixate on life's dilemmas and dogmas; there can be no dispute in relation to principles as a righteous, unpolluted conscience knows what is decent and what is not! In America you will not find the writhing of weak souls decaying due to an absence of principles and a boundless desire for gratification — for as much gratification as possible, at the least possible cost, preferably at no cost at all, bar the cost of their own debasement. While in Europe the main stimulus for action is gratification, in America it is the desire to achieve something, to close the deal, to leave a mark. Breaking a record is an honour, raising yourself up — the aim.

In Europe they imagine that "liberating yourself" from all rules and putting your "self" on a pedestal as the only aim and highest authority constitutes strength and truth; here that signifies only weakness with respect to one's desires and the atrophy of "free will". American society is free, as it both understands how and wishes of its own free choice (*liberum arbitrium*) to master the desires and weaknesses of human nature and to honestly assess and reject any sophistry prompted by its own weaknesses. The motto of my late father (author of the book *Upadek Europy*) '*In voluntate – libertas, in libertate – salus!*'[8] (In will – freedom, in freedom – salvation!) holds true here. Moral laws are as absolute as the laws of physics. Anyone not accepting them will inexorably and inevitably be crushed — they have miscalculated.

In America the fundamental might of humans backed by the immense power of their will is combined with a flair for finding practical solutions. The famed practicality of Americans in effect consists of the direct transfer of thoughts into action, of theory into practice.

America reminds one of the might of Rome as it developed: first of all it focused on existence and safety, it built up its own internal strength, created laws and ruled. Rome took its science from Egypt and its philosophy and art from Greece, just as America took these from Europe. The Romans were a clear-headed, practical nation which looked to its own advantage like America, although ethically Americans stand incomparably higher than the imperialist, egotistical Romans. So in spite of myself the following question comes to mind: 'With respect to America might Europe play the role once played by Greece?'

* * *

Americans also have their negative characteristics. Accusations of bribery are widespread in America (they call it graft). As I did not settle permanently in any one place I could not personally verify this matter which is covert by its very nature. The following comments are based on what I have been told by people who are permanently resident in the United States and on my own observations of what is visible on the surface.

On the topic of bribery associated with elections to legislative bodies I was informed that running in such elections does indeed cost a great deal because of canvassing, advertisements, venues for hustings etc. These costs are covered by the party. I was also told votes cannot be bought as every citizen takes too active an interest in the government's policies; the government is viewed as an agent mandated by the voters and a Congressman as genuinely representing voters' needs and convictions. Voters maintain active contact with "their Congressman" or their State's Senator by means of periodicals, letters and personal interventions. The majority of citizens belong to organised political parties and try to get candidates who match their political persuasion elected. During my stay in America a magazine uncovered the fact that Senator L. had bribed some voters. A real storm blew up in all the periodicals and public opinion was as outraged as it could possibly be.

I heard no reports of bribery for the purpose of securing lucrative positions; I never heard any complaints about irregularity in the way official institutions functioned or of any "unofficial expenditure" required to get a matter resolved, even though I continually came into contact with people who had dealings with these institutions, and I also had contact with neighbours etc. Reputedly instances of bribery occur more frequently among the police than elsewhere, especially in New York.

Periodicals have even more power in America than in Europe; they serve specific parties or aims and often, to gain popularity, they run campaigns against abuses or any sort of dishonesty by officials. However, before they can raise this type of issue they have to conduct an exceedingly meticulous investigation on their own account and gather evidence proving their case beyond doubt. This is because in the event of losing defamation proceedings in court, the periodical might face a fine which could bankrupt the mightiest of journals and send its editors and reporters to prison. The judge does not apply fixed levels of fines as the statute does not set any: a judge can take into account the particulars of the case and their own views and determine the amount of a fine relative to the office held by the injured party and the means of the culprit. This is an extension of the prerogative of a juror in a criminal case to a civil matter.

I have the following experience to note with regard to business relationships. My task was to introduce my sugar beet seeds to the American market. In many European countries competing companies try to maintain the "goodwill connected to their brand" by paying appropriate "commission" to certain dependable persons. In the process of organising my business I made enquiries as to what was done in American sugar factories in this respect. The people I entrusted with my affairs explained to me that with the exception of a few people, whose names I was given, this route was not followed. Sure enough in the course of several years of material transactions not once has any of my agents given me a bill for "additional expenditure" of that type. It gives me pleasure to note that in Poland too all is well in this respect.

In America I have also not encountered the practice of "offering contributions" to various public officials which is common in Europe. Even "gratuities" are very limited, especially in the west.

Typically Americans are extravagant and wasteful in all areas of life. Their work is often swift, but slapdash. It is worth highlighting the exceptionally extensive methods of exploitation and the wastage of natural resources — it is literally a pillage and plunder economy. A vast and exceptionally rich country was discovered, it came under the control of the white race and was left at its mercy. The Europeans showed no mercy and ransacked everything: they drove out the American Indians, they decimated the glorious herds of bison, they felled so much forest that the government now has to take measures to protect the country's woodlands. They acted like a person who chops down a tree to make it easier to pick the fruit.

The intellectual aspect of American life has taken an appropriate direction: it has taken on the marked characteristics of practicality. Science, art and literature are poorly developed here, even though science has achieved wide popular appeal among all sections of the general public. The American's constant toil to gain material wealth might well make a European feel weary. However it is understandable that a nation which is brimming with energy and has at its fingertips the vast resources provided by nature's abundance, yet lacks the strife between ethnic, political and religious groups and has extremely restricted scope for diplomatic careers, has focused all its energy on the practicalities of life and in this has found an outlet for the growth and enterprise of individuals. The conjunction of two factors which are so rarely in harmony with each other has shaped the psyche of the modern American: on the one hand clear-headed realism and practicality, on the other youthful idealism and deep religiousness.

* * *

Religious sentiment is as well developed here as indifferentism and gross materialism in, say, France or Germany. Americans' piety is sincere and deep. It is without a doubt their need for quiet reflection, for acknowledging religious truths, and for a spiritual life that brings them to the churches. To realise this, one only needs to see how widely Sundays are celebrated and how full the churches are, even in the afternoon. Young artisans, labourers, people from higher social strata, all hasten to deepen their spiritual life and to quietly reflect. The impression is that this holy day truly consists of spiritual reflection and distancing oneself from the mundane tasks of daily life in order to focus on developing the spiritual aspect of one's existence and one's labours.

There are an inordinate number of churches. I am told that in New York, the city closest in character to European cities, there are nearly 1,000 churches and chapels, despite a significant percentage of Jewish residents. The ratio of church buildings to population is the same in this enormous, modern city as in Kraków, an ancient city whose development has been constrained.

There is a whole array of religious meetings and church services. In hotels, a list of church services on forthcoming holy days is permanently on display. In many places there is a Bible in every hotel room. In the mountains one comes across excerpts from the Bible and the Epistles carved into the rocks in large letters.

The customary payment of 10 cents on entering a church (or more if one wishes) may seem strange to us; however, its purpose is to avoid collections interrupting church services. In poor parishes, e.g. one of the outlying Polish parishes in New York with about 500 parishioners, such a collection raises

40 – 50 dollars a time. When a special collection for rebuilding was announced in one of the larger churches, 100,000 dollars was raised on a single Sunday. Each person feels they have a duty to contribute at least a small offering.

The behaviour of the general public in churches is exemplary. There is none of that looking around, pushing past others and strolling about: people do not arrive late for services and they do not leave at whatever point suits them. Proselytising and championing one's faith are highly developed phenomena, but naturally they are conducted with respect for other people's beliefs.

A religious strand is a fundamental characteristic of the social system and of the American's soul. The larger waves of emigration to North America started in times of religious persecution: whether it was the Huguenots or Protestants or Catholics or the Puritans with their severe interpretations of religion or finally the Mennonites who were persecuted in Russia in the XIX Century — all of these people were fanatically attached to their own religion and preferred to leave their country rather than renounce their faith! The numerous sects in existence and the new ones that continue to spring up are evidence of the lively interest in religious affairs. In the constitutions of the first States there is a very marked religious element which underpins their laws. So, for example, the wording of the profession of faith for members of the House of Representatives and government officials in Pennsylvania is: 'I do believe in one God, the creator and governor of the universe, the rewarder of the good and the punisher of the wicked. And I do acknowledge the Scriptures of the Old and New Testament to be given by Divine inspiration.'[9]

In Delaware it is: 'I do profess faith in God the Father, and in Jesus Christ His only Son, and in the Holy Ghost, one God, blessed for evermore; and I do acknowledge the holy scriptures of the Old and New Testament to be given by divine inspiration.'[10]

In South Carolina the following articles had to be signed: '1st. That there is one eternal God, and a future state of rewards and punishments. 2d. That God is publicly to be worshipped. 3d. That the Christian religion is the true religion. 4th. That the holy scriptures of the Old and New Testaments are of divine inspiration, and are the rule of faith and practice.'[11]

The question of separation between church and state was resolved in America by allowing churches complete independence from the state — churches are dependent upon and exclusively maintained by their own adherents. The question of the marriage ceremony was resolved in a very practical way with no ill effect on the faith groups which existed in America. A betrothed couple has an obligation to appear before a judge who grants them permission to enter into matrimony on the basis of documents or personal statements confirmed by oath. The couple then take this license to the cleric of their choice or to the civil authorities. The person officiating, whether clergy or laity, has an obligation to inform the judge that the marriage has taken place so that the judge can record it in the official register.

* * *

It is common knowledge that women have a privileged position in America. Law, custom and public opinion all come to the defence of women. Women are respected and protected by everyone. I met two young women who were making a journey from Oklahoma to San Francisco on foot for a wager i.e. walking a distance of about 3,000 km.

It was explained to me that they were not in any danger, as everyone would feel it their duty to both extend a helping hand and protect them; as soon as a man noticed anyone pestering them the culprit 'would get a black eye'. Women also have a great deal of freedom. Family life, which is a strong institution in America, is their main responsibility. Women who are not married work in factories, but only perform light duties.

Courts pronounce extremely severe sentences in cases where the "marital promise" is broken. In these cases, as with defamation, the judge has the power to determine the level of compensation according to the wealth and social standing of the parties.

Prostitution occurs of course, but it is not tolerated by the law; neither does the law tolerate cohabitation. All forms of pornography are strictly forbidden; indeed there is no pornography as the public do not find it to their taste. The shocking theatre performances which young women frequent back home are not tolerated in America, neither by law nor by all-powerful public opinion — its guardians may even go as far as boxing a person's ears to back up their principles.

Women who travel to the United States alone have to reveal who will host them. If a woman does not have any friends or acquaintances with whom she can stay, the police will take care of her and make sure she is not led astray. A certain elegant Parisian lady travelled to New York by ship in 1st class and on arrival was asked by the authorities where she was headed. She replied that she was going to stay with a gentleman friend.

'Are you marrying him?' asked the official. 'What business is that of yours?' retorted the French lady. She was not allowed onto American soil: she was sent to the barracks on Ellis Island and from there she returned to Europe. Other women, who claimed they were on their way to their fiancé to get married, were also dispatched back to Europe once it transpired they were cohabiting.

One particularity is that anyone who already has a contract for work in the United States is not allowed onto American soil. The purpose of this rule is to prevent workers being shipped into the United States on exploitative contracts; another reason is that everyone present in the territory of the United States must be a free agent. Even an accompanying maid or a child's nursemaid cannot be declared as a servant, but has to be declared as a fellow-traveller.

On coming ashore every person is obliged to show they have at least 25 dollars in their possession; the point of this is to avoid the potential exploitation of workers without the means to live from their own resources for a period of time or to travel far into the interior of the country.

* * *

Those who say that idealism is absent in American society are mistaken. They are idealists and dogmatists. An American does not philosophise, yet the simplicity of his honest judgements make his world view more sagacious than that of many European philosophers and statesmen, who are led down the wrong path by doctrine or arrogance. On the continent idealism is just a form of adornment for degenerates; here the idealism is full-blooded and bursting with vigour. Americans have a great deal of sincere enthusiasm and genuine idealism, not apathetic idealism which is only for show (to oneself or to others), but idealism which forms the basis for a life with real meaning.

Rather than losing them in the course of their everyday commonplace struggles, Americans strive with all their might to implement their ideals in their lives. And their might is considerable because will, self-control, self-direction and self-discipline are an American's main aspirations.

It is a genuinely youthful society, full of verve, nobleness and aspirations; an idealistic society, but not one with its head in the clouds. One is struck above all by their great dignity and probity, which is deeply ingrained and entails certain obligations.

A real cult of freedom does not leave room in the American's soul for servitude in any shape or form; in the event of any impositions on his way of life that were contrary to his convictions, an American's self-respect and personal dignity would rouse him to resist with all his strength. An American would rather die fighting than submit to violation of his dignity and his principles.

* * *

Beyond the wide Rocky Mountain range a strange landscape stretches out all the way to the Sierra Nevada mountain chain: a plateau 5,000 to 6,000 feet above sea level; pitiful rivers without any outlet to the sea discharging into salt lakes; a landscape similar to Doré's drawings of the desert in the Bible. This is the State of Utah. After a long journey through the desert, oases appear, then cultivated fields and finally the salt lakes. This is where the Mormons settled after they left Illinois in 1846 as a result of the persecution they experienced. After one and a half years travelling through prairies, mountains and deserts the first wagon train of barely a few hundred people stopped here. They were led by Brigham Young, a powerful personality. While endeavouring to establish settlements and create the conditions for civilised life to develop, they came up against colossal obstacles in this wild land a thousand miles away from the civilised world. The difficulties can be seen from the fact that they used wooden nails since there were no iron ones available and the cost of importing a pound of nails was one dollar. It was a lifestyle similar to Robinson Crusoe's, but in a group. With incredible energy and perseverance the new settlers transformed desolate desert into pockets of civilised life. Mining, manufacturing and agriculture have developed extremely well here. A few large sugar factories developed successfully in the State of Utah and its neighbour Idaho. I found kindly support there and a very correct attitude to business, which hasn't changed to this day, so I established my fields for growing sugar beet seeds alongside these sugar factories.

Mormonism has 300,000 believers. Their ecclesiastical organisation is extremely strong. Proselytism is highly developed. During the period when the Mormon sect promoted the principle of polygamy, the land they inhabited, Utah, was treated as a Territory of the United States and so did not benefit from the privileges accorded to a State. In the end the Mormons were forced to abolish polygamy and subsequently they joined the federation and gained the entitlements of a State. To this day they have preserved their religion which is a mixture of the

Christian faith, traditions taken from the Old Testament and the ideas of the founder of this sect, J. Smith, who is considered to be a prophet (as declared by Smith himself in about the year 1830).

The most important city in the whole region is Salt Lake City, also called Zion by the Mormons, which lies on the river Jordan and has a population of about 100,000. The Temple, a magnificent building of white granite, is inaccessible to people of other faiths and even believers are only allowed to enter in specific circumstances. The Tabernacle, a peculiar building constructed mainly of wood and shaped like a barrel cut in half longways, serves as a meeting place which everyone has the right to enter. It can hold 10,000 people. This is where you can find the famous pipe organ, said to be the largest and most beautiful organ in the world. Listening to the music flowing from this organ you are convinced it is a concert performed by an orchestra, choirs and soloists with powerful voices; you have the impression that you can distinguish the words of the songs.

A causeway tens of kilometres long leads westwards from Salt Lake City, over the Great Salt Lake in the direction of the Nevada desert and California. Entire forests were cut down to build it. This allowed the railway route, which originally went around the lake, to be shortened. The Great Salt Lake is more than ten times larger than Lake Geneva. The concentration of salt in the lake's water is 25%.

This massive dead sea (120 km in length) makes a very strong impression: it is surrounded by bare, austere mountains with sandy hillocks at their feet and in the midst of this lifeless landscape — irrigated valleys covered in luxuriant vegetation.

The State of Idaho also has a plateau at a high elevation, but the landscape turns mountainous as one moves north. The renowned Yellowstone National Park is situated on the borders of Idaho, Montana and Wyoming; it is the largest of what are known as National Parks. These Parks are the property of the nation (i.e. of the Union) and are therefore managed by the federal government. Yellowstone National Park covers a rectangular area 100 km long by 86 km wide. It is a place of amazing wonders with abundant natural riches. The wooded wilderness, wild mountains, numerous waterfalls and geysers all contribute to a genuinely fantastical beauty spot which still remains in its original state, untouched. It is not permitted to dig any mines or set up home or to hunt here. All animals can live safely in the Park without being harassed by humans; in return even the numerous bears and wild cattle do not attack humans here. However, nature's purity has been tainted by roads built through previously inaccessible places, which vehicles and omnibuses travel along regularly to enable tourists to visit the area. Permanent campsites have also been set up with tents where one can stay the night and obtain nourishment. Still, anyone who wishes to experience nature in its completely untamed form can easily find nearby virgin forests and mountains so wild they may even starve to death if their provisions run out, unless they can successfully hunt food. Sometimes a ground squirrel or gopher can save a person from starvation. Sometimes a hunter, lured by a rustling in the undergrowth and expecting to find a rabbit, is bitten by a rattlesnake.

* * *

California is a good example of the extent to which those who run a country are the deciding factor in the level of development and civilisation achieved. Back when Spaniards ruled the region it was known as the Great Californian Desert. In 1848 Mexico voluntarily ceded California to the United States in a treaty, along with the huge desert lands to the east right up to the Rocky Mountains (Nevada, Arizona and Utah). A year later huge gold deposits were discovered in California and the Californian Gold Rush began. Hordes of people made their way to the Far West through boundless, wild lands. On their way many of these expeditions fought with American Indians and battled with even more dangerous prairie fires, as they crossed arid deserts, mighty rivers and treacherous mountain chains. The following story comes from those times. One member of an expedition making its way west murdered another person from the group. The summary court sentenced him to expulsion from the camp without weapons or food. For a long time the convict trailed along close to the track which his group was following: he was vulnerable to all sorts of dangers in that wild country and near death from hunger and hardship. The expedition to which he belonged took a wrong turn in the Sierra Nevada mountains and was caught out by snow and attacked by Red Indians; their food supplies ran out and they were facing certain death. The banished man saw this and struggled on over the mountain ridge to inform a distant White settlement. Help arrived and the expedition was rescued.

Today's California is rightly considered one of the richest lands in the world. Market gardening, agriculture and industry have developed in an unprecedented way there.

The surface area of California is 400,000 km^2, so it is significantly larger than Austria (not including Hungary) which covers an area of 300,000 km^2. The population of California was: 50,000 in 1850; 380,000 in 1860; 1,500,000 in 1900; and 2,400,000 in 1910.

In the decade from 1900 to 1910 the population grew by 60%. In the same period the population of the United States grew by 21%. In some other States the population grew even faster e.g. Idaho by 101%, Oklahoma by 110% and Washington State (on the shores of the Pacific Ocean, not to be confused with the city Washington) by 120%. The lowest growth in population at this time, around the 5% level, occurred in the smaller States in the east. However New York State, whose surface area was 125,000 km^2 (over 1½ times larger than Galicia), had 76 inhabitants per km^2 (Galicia had 102 per km^2 in 1910) and population growth of 25%. Recall that in the same decade the population of Austria only grew by 9%.

It is almost exclusively the coastal area of California between the Sierra Nevada mountains and the Pacific Ocean that is inhabited. The interior of the country is taken up by mountains and deserts.

California's output covers a broad range of goods. Here are a few figures relating to the year 1914.

They produced:

Cereal crops (wheat, barley, oats, maize, rye) amounting to $167 m., or $67 = 335 kr. per capita (in Galicia output of these cereal crops was on average about 60 kr. per capita).

Potatoes with a value of $15 m., or $6 = 30 kr. per capita (approximately the same as in Galicia).

Hay (mainly baled lucerne, called alfalfa over here) with a value of $90 m.
Dried fruit (raisins, prunes, peaches, apricots, figs, apples) 2 m. metric cwt. or 20,000 wagons.
Almonds and nuts 100,000 metric cwt. or 1,000 wagons.
Olives 250,000 metric cwt. or 2,500 wagons.
Butter 270,000 metric cwt. or 2,700 wagons (according to the statistics the price of butter is 3 krone per kg).
Cheese 27,000 metric cwt. or 270 wagons (the price according to the statistics is 1.75 kr. per kg).
Honey 17,000 metric cwt. or 170 wagons.
Sugar from sugar beet 1,520,000 metric cwt. or 15,200 wagons i.e. 60 kg per capita.

In Austria the sugar production per capita was 30 kg, while in Galicia it was 2 kg per capita.

The largest sugar factories in the world, such as Spreckels and Oxnard, can be found in California. The latter ran a campaign in 1911 which showed the average sugar content of the beet harvested was 21¼%. In Europe the result is considered to be excellent if the average sugar concentration is 15%.

Exported **oranges and lemons** amounted to 56,000 wagons.

The value of **metal and mineral production** was 43 m., of which 20 m. relates to gold.

The figures for the value of **crude oil production** are $50 m. = 250 m. kr., or 100 kr. per capita (in Galicia the value of petroleum production is 44 m. kr., or 5.50 kr. per capita).

It is astonishing and seems quite improbable that plant cultivation in this rich Californian coastal area is highly successful, even without any irrigation, despite the fact that literally no rain falls over the whole summer. The scanty rains only fall from December until the beginning of March. This success can be explained by the natural subirrigation that occurs: the water comes from underground streams which flow from the neighbouring mountains where the rainfall is particularly abundant. Both the cloudy skies (usually overcast until midday) and the abundant dew help the plants to do without rain.

The only traces left of Spanish rule in the western United States are the numerous Spanish geographical names. The current influx of Mexicans is the worst element of the population and they are the shoddiest workers.

* * *

I visited the valley of the Mariposas River in California where those giants of the plant world the sequoias grow: they are taller than the tower of St Mary's in Kraków and over 6,000 years old. These trees were discovered over 60 years ago by an American who named them in honour of his university colleague the Red Indian Sequoiah. On the way I had a conversation with the guide who saddled and looked after my horse. I questioned him as to why these plants, which have such strong life force and produce seeds which can grow into trees even in Europe, seemed to have such poor reproductive capability (hardly any young sequoias could be seen). My groom replied, 'Who are we to know the laws governing life? We only know the laws of...' 'The laws of death,' I interjected. 'No, we do not know the laws of death either! We know that after our death the body will decay, but not the soul. My body is nothing more than a garment that I wear. The only laws we do know are the laws of mathematics; we know they are not just a figment of the human imagination — astronomy proves it!' The man who reasoned in this way worked tending horses in a hotel throughout the summer and during the winter worked in San Francisco doing minor electrical engineering jobs.

Spiritual refinement encompasses the full breadth of American society.

* * *

America owes its astonishing cultural and economic development not just to abundant natural resources, as in this respect it ranks behind other countries e.g. Russia, but also to the unhindered development of its society, the direction of all its energy towards productive work and finally the moral qualities of its people.

The social and political system of the United States is a spontaneous creation; it is a form of political life that has been created by the nation for itself; the constitution came into being through the will of the people and it is shaped by their needs. By creating this constitution American society aimed to protect its own interests and its own happiness, and it achieved this aim.

The conceptual framework of this political system was guided by: love of freedom, respect for the individual both in legislation and amongst the people, and a deep religiousness.

The immortal Washington, to whom America owes its liberation, saw his role as serving the nation. Once he had fulfilled his task he relinquished power despite the nation's pleas and wishes. In his admirably straightforward farewell address he set out clear guidelines for the way forward to be followed henceforth by the federal government. Lincoln defined the system of government in words which live on in the soul of every citizen of the United States: 'government of the people, by the people, for the people!'[12] The preamble to the Constitution expresses the same sentiment: 'We the People of the United States do ordain and establish this Constitution!'[13]

Only the fundamental statutes guaranteed by a common constitution are binding throughout the United States, so the laws in individual States do vary greatly from State to State. However they all share a common fundamental approach and are harmonious in their entirety. Thus individual States are able to introduce an official language other than English in their own State, but they can not implement, let's say, an insignificant law that is at odds with the Constitution. A customs union without any interstate limitations covers the whole territory of the United States.

In 1861 a great war broke out between the northern and southern States over the fundamental concepts underpinning the federal constitution. The southerners wanted to uphold the institution of Negro slavery and since Congress could not sanction that principle the southern States decided to break away. This was contrary to the principle of a union of all States based on a mutually accepted constitution. Hence it was a war of secession. It was about upholding the principles of the Constitution and maintaining unity. This bitter war lasted almost 4 years. It was as if this war, which was in effect the only one in 130 years of the United States' existence, was an atonement for the sins of generations which had used whips to seize Negroes from their homes and halters when driving them to work.

The Northern States were victorious and so the principle of human freedom and the concept of unity prevailed. The war was not followed by repression so the previously prevailing harmony soon returned.

The American Constitution guarantees freedom of conscience, freedom of the press and freedom of speech. It distinguishes three branches of authority: legislative, executive and judicial.

1. Legislative power rests with Congress which is made up of the House of Representatives and the Senate. Members of the House of Representatives are elected directly by the people in each State and the number of Representatives for each State depends on the size of its population. Each State's legislative body elects two Senators for a term of 6 years.
2. Executive power is in the hands of the President who implements the law through his officials and potentially also by means of the army; the President is the Commander-in-Chief of the armed forces, but Congress decides whether to declare war. The President is chosen for a term of 4 years by the electors of all the States. Any citizen of the United States born in America can be elected as President. Americans value this right very highly, not because any person really could become President, but for the sake of the principle.
3. Judicial authority rests with the courts of law set up by Congress and with the Supreme Court, which sits in the central part of the building housing the House of Representatives in one wing and the Senate in the other. The role of the Supreme Court is to be the guardian of the Constitution: it has the power to overturn any statute which

conflicts with the Constitution, whether it is a statute enacted by an individual State or a federal statute ratified by the President. Every citizen has the right to file a claim in a lower court requesting revocation of any particular law. The instant the Supreme Court rules that a particular law violates the Constitution, that law is null and void throughout the United States. Similar principles form the basis for legislation in each State. The Constitution does not tolerate any unethical laws, such as laws allowing polygamy. While the Mormons practised polygamy their land was treated as a Territory and did not have the rights accorded to a State. In a similar way anarchism is an unlawful doctrine. It is not only people becoming United States citizens that have to make a written declaration stating they do not subscribe to anarchic doctrines nor practise polygamy: every single traveller must do so before setting foot in the New World. In the event of any misdemeanour the person will be held responsible on two fronts: for the offence and also for making a false statement. Some years ago an anarchist grouping was formed in Chicago which carried out a politically motivated attack. People who had not taken part in the attack but had brought it about by their propaganda were held responsible to a greater extent than the perpetrators. They were charged and it was proven they were morally responsible for the attack, so they were hanged.

It is well known that the federal army is raised by recruitment; it works on the basis of five-year contracts. Soldiers are provided with uniforms, excellent food and accommodation and in addition receive $30 pay a month. Beyond the gates of their barracks soldiers wear civilian clothes as uniforms are not a popular sight. Even the generals take their uniforms with them in a small handheld trunk when they travel out of the city to military exercises. Apart from the federal army every State has a volunteer unpaid militia which holds exercises from time to time. It is a generally accepted patriotic custom that members of the militia are released from their private occupations for the hours or days required for these exercises. These militamen also do not put on their uniforms until they are at their exercises. The militia is not only called up when military action is required (generally an exceedingly rare occurrence), but also when natural disasters occur in order to provide assistance.

* * *

I heard an account of American relations with Cuba from a man of Polish-Jewish heritage who had lived there during the period when America was at war with Spain. This man had been brought up in France yet still treasured with the utmost reverence mementos of 1863 taken out of Poland by his father. He also showed me a history of Poland published in the French language and portraits of Reytan and Kościuszko.

He was one of the insurgents who had fought against the tyranny of the Spaniards and their exploitation of Cuba and its population, which lived in extreme poverty. Following the arrival of the United States army to support the insurgents and the subsequent yielding of the Spaniards, the Americans set to organising the country and introducing order. During the period of Spanish rule yellow fever had plagued Cuba, continually reaping innumerable victims. The Americans could see this contagious disease was spread by mosquitoes so they wiped them out by covering the surfaces of all bodies of stagnant water with a very thin layer of oil. They burnt down the miserable, dirty houses along with their furnishings, paying handsome compensation for everything. The result was astounding; within two years yellow fever had been eradicated. What was once a dangerous epidemic turned into sporadic occurrences of the disease with the fatality rate reducing to improbably low numbers in comparison to the previous incidence. It was the start of a period in which Cuba flourished to an unprecedented extent. After the war ended, the insurgent I met had opened a shop selling food and soon built up capital of about 30,000 francs, but he was robbed of his money during a bout of illness after contracting yellow fever. Instead of taking this to heart, he left Cuba and moved to the United States; he was working there as a domestic in a hotel (earning about $100 a month) for the time being, but naturally his intention was to start up an independent business in the near future to once again earn his way to an independent existence. It is well known that a few years after occupying Cuba the Americans departed, leaving Cuba with a government of its own and independence.

Today Cuba is an independent republic and benefits from certain privileges when exporting its goods to the United States. The Cubans attempted to join the Union, but no agreement was reached. It seems the Americans were wary of excessive imports of Cuban goods competing with their own goods and besides that did not want to let a racially alien and less civilised group into their federation.

* * *

To understand Americans it is helpful to familiarise oneself with the theories put forward by Roosevelt, that eminent and popular American statesman. Roosevelt was raised to the highest office as a result of his principles which reflected the American way of thinking, his battle against corruption and his campaign against trusts. In his later years his progressive stance was undermined by the imperialistic, partly nationalistic, policies he wanted introduced. In a collection of essays entitled *American Ideals* Roosevelt expounds his political theories which are based on high-mindedness, courage, strenuous effort and fair play.

Here are some extracts from the aforementioned work:

'We rightfully value success, but sometimes we overvalue it, for we tend to forget that success may be obtained by means which should make it abhorred and despised by every honorable man.

'One section of the community deifies as "smartness" the kind of trickery which enables a man without conscience to succeed in the financial or political world. Another section of the community deifies violent homicidal lawlessness. If ever our people as a whole adopt these views, then we shall have proved that we are unworthy of the heritage our forefathers left us; and our country will go down in ruin.'[14]

'No bandit community of the Middle Ages can have led a more unlovely life than would be the life of men to whom trade and manufactures were everything, and to whom such words as national honor and glory, as courage and daring, and loyalty and unselfishness, had become meaningless. The merely material, the merely commercial ideal, the ideal of the men "whose fatherland is the till" is in its very essence debasing and lowering. It is as true now as ever it was that no man and no nation shall live by bread alone.'[15]

'The worst foes of America are the foes to that orderly liberty without which our Republic must speedily perish. The reckless labor agitator who arouses the mob to riot and bloodshed is the most dangerous of the workingman's enemies.'[16]

'The man who is content to let politics go from bad to worse, jesting at the corruption of politicians, the man who is content to see the maladministration of justice without an immediate effort to reform it, is shirking his duty and is preparing the way for infinite woe in the future.'[17]

'People who are unable to appreciate any quality that is not a mercantile commodity, who do not understand that a poet may do far more for a country than the owner of a factory producing nails, who do not realize that no amount of commercial prosperity can supply the lack of the heroic virtues, or can in itself solve the terrible social problems.'[18]

'The mere materialist is, above all things, shortsighted. To men of a certain kind, trade and property are far more sacred than life or honor, of far more consequence than the great thoughts and lofty emotions, which alone make a nation mighty.'[19]

Roosevelt is not a pacifist. His politics are the politics of expansion, even of aggression to a certain extent, but he promotes fairness, honesty and the use of honourable means in politics with very marked insistence. Let's glance at the principles he propounds in his collection of essays entitled: *The Strenuous Life*.

He praises active virtues: energy, valour and resilience.

He suggests individuals should aim to strive, to battle, to forge ahead and to gain victory. 'We admire the man who embodies victorious effort; the man who never wrongs his neighbor, who is prompt to help a friend, but who has those virile qualities necessary to win.'[20]

Of family life he says, 'The man must be glad to do a man's work, to dare and endure and to labor. The woman must be the housewife, the helpmeet of the homemaker, the wise and fearless mother of many healthy children.'[21]

Referring to France he says, 'When men fear work or fear righteous war, when women fear motherhood, they stand on the brink of damnation and are fit subjects for scorn. A nation that adheres to such norms is rotten to the heart's core.'[22]

On public life he says, 'Let us therefore be both honest and brave, to serve high ideals, yet to use practical methods.'[23]

'Bodily vigor is good, and vigor of intellect is even better, but far above both is character.'[24]

'Any public man should remember that the cardinal points in his doctrine ought to be the Seventh and Eighth Commandments.'[25]

'Absolute honesty is a fundamental of healthy political life. We can afford to differ on duties, tariffs, domestic and foreign policy, but we cannot afford to differ on the question of honesty if we expect our republic permanently to endure. Honesty is an absolute prerequisite to efficient service to the public. Unless a man is honest in public life we have no right to keep him, it matters not how brilliant his capacity.'[26]

'"Liar" is just as ugly a word as "thief". There is no difference between perjury and mendacity in the sphere of moral concepts. According to the law of morality and righteousness, he is precisely as guilty if, instead of lying in a court, he lies in a newspaper or on the stump; and in all probability the evil effects of his conduct are more pernicious.'[27]

In foreign affairs his focus was to broaden the scope of those factors driving the development of the United States which have made it a powerful and happy nation.

Cannon, the Speaker of the House of Representatives for many years, expressed the same thought at a banquet held in honour of the unveiling of the Kościuszko and Pułaski monuments: 'My wish for Europe is that it may become the United States. By this I do not mean the United States might take over Europe, but that I hope our principles will take root there and that the European states create for themselves the same sort of harmonious existence we enjoy throughout the enormous continent covered by our federation.'

According to Roosevelt the guiding principles for good organisation are to find people of character, select appropriate positions to match their talents and give them a wide remit.

* * *

In order to understand the situation in the United States one needs to be aware of the following: it is a country almost as big as the whole of Europe including the European part of Russia; in terms of topography and climate it has every category except the subtropical and arctic climates; its population density vacillates between extremes of 90 inhabitants per km^2 (in the eastern States), matching the population density of Austria, and just under 1 inhabitant per km^2 in Montana, Wyoming, Nevada and Arizona i.e. an area the size of Austro-Hungary and Germany put together; the law varies significantly between States even though the underlying legal framework is identical.

Despite this the American spirit remains unchanged in all circumstances.

It is instructive to juxtapose certain statistics when comparing Europe with America.

The annual **death rate** per thousand inhabitants was 27 in Europe (including Russia), 23 in Austria and 15 in the United States.

The number of **suicides** a year per 100,000 inhabitants was 10 in England, 16 in the United States, 18 in Austro-Hungary, 21 in Germany and 23 in France.

The number of **lunatics** per 100,000 inhabitants was 143 in the United States, 235 in France and 328 in England.

The population of the United States amounted to 5½ million in 1800 compared to 76 million in 1900; in effect it rose fifteenfold in a period when the population barely doubled in Europe. Currently the population of the United States is over 100 million.

Between 1880 and 1900 emigration to the United States amounted to just under half a million people a year, whereas between 1905 and 1912 it grew to almost one million a year. The largest number of emigrants come from Austria, followed by Russia and Italy.

National wealth was assessed at:

United States .... 650 million krone
Germany .... 300 " "
Austro-Hungary .... 125 " "
Russia .... 200 " "

The average wealth per capita amounted to:

in the United States (in 1904)	6,500 krone
in Germany	4,600 "
in Austro-Hungary	2,500 "
in Russia	1,300 "

The growth in the national wealth of the United States is shown by the following figures:

in 1880	total	assets	per	capita	2,400 kr.
in 1890	"	"	"	"	4,800 kr.
in 1900	"	"	"	"	5,800 kr.
in 1904	"	"	"	"	6,500 kr.

* * *

The utter dissimilarity between the Old and New Worlds along with the multitude of tasks faced by Americans result in them taking little interest in Europe; even the feuds in European domestic politics only find a faint echo in the newspapers here. Americans look on from outside and do not really understand what these people want from each other and what it is that makes them unwilling or unable to live as Our Lord commanded.

Life in America is fundamentally different to life in Europe; one honestly feels as if European ways were something that existed a long time ago in distant history.

In the United States the state leaves society to take care of satisfying its own needs. The state declines to undertake all activities which could be carried out through the initiative of individuals or by private action and tries to restrict itself to a supporting role, as it has little faith that a bureaucracy is capable of performing the work. Thus, for example, not just the railways, but also the telephone services, telegraph systems etc. are private entities in America. Similarly hospitals, higher education establishments, scientific institutions, insurers etc. exist thanks to the enterprise of individuals or associations. The state avoids any coercion of its citizens and tries to minimise government intervention; by working on the assumption that adults should not be mollycoddled it develops individuals who venture bravely into life and have a sense of responsibility. On the assumption that life is a better teacher than doctrine and that people themselves are best placed to judge what they need, the state does not impose on society laws devised arbitrarily by theoreticians or people driven by a desire for power. This is the outcome of significantly differing ideas in Europe and America regarding the role of the state. Whereas in Europe statehood developed along a path of subordinating individuals to the aims of the state and in modern times is moving towards a system where everything is absorbed into a socialist state, in America the state is subordinated to the interests of the populace and its political system is a manifestation of individualistic development. This stands in stark contrast to treating society as a collective, which, even in the supposedly progressive currents of socialism and communism, tends towards restricting the freedom of individuals and eliminating any differences between them.

The prototype for the European social order is the form of statehood given firm foundations by the Byzantine emperors Constantine and Justinian, whereas America developed its political system based on concepts taken from Christian democracy, natural philosophy and English Congregationalism.

One often comes across the opinion that American society is free because it has become mature enough to be free. There is some truth in this since social virtues are indeed the route to freedom, but no nation can mature while it is in bondage nor improve itself while enslaved. My late father clarified this thought with the analogy of waiting until the fruit had ripened to carry an orange tree out into the sun — a flawed idea.

In my presentation of America's characteristics I have tried to capture the main features, those that are typical. The overall picture is positive. The conclusion to draw is not that in America God's kingdom has materialised on Earth nor that their society is made up of saints, but that in terms of moral and practical qualities Americans undeniably rank much higher than Europeans. On this sort of background negative phenomena stand out more distinctly and are easily and eagerly pointed out.

* * *

After writing these notes I happened to come across a book called *The Spirit of America* written by van Dyke, a professor at Princeton University. I was astonished to see an uncanny correspondence between my own observations and arguments and the analysis presented by this undoubted expert on the American way of life. His description of Americans as 'a people of idealists engaged in a great practical task'[28] strikes me as very apt.

I have recently studied Sienkiewicz's '*Szkice Amerykańskie*'[29] (Letter VI) and I find his views about American society generally match my own observations.

After returning from America I also read some older predictions about how the United States would develop.

They have come true, so it is worth quoting them. Shortly after the Congress of Vienna the eminent German historian K. von Rotteck wrote in his book *Allgemeine Geschichte*, 'In the youthful New World **natural rational law** is fashioning a rare world power. In North America it has already sunk deep roots, it has already borne the most splendid fruit. All human history has not produced a single example of such quick, such salutary, such wondrous forward progress as we see in the "free States" of North America.'[30] In the mid-XIX Century Ph. Chasles, a member of the French Academy and a professor at the Collège de France wrote, 'As Europe disintegrates, America takes shape.' and 'America is on the rise, Europe is passing away.'[31] (*Etudes sur les hommes et les mœurs au XIX siècle*).

Stefan Buszczyński, the author of the book *Ameryka i Europa* published in 1876, showed astounding intuition in understanding the American spirit. Loving one's neighbour and freedom, values embedded in an American's soul, are derived from the Christian principles on which the political system of the United States was built. My father expressed it thus: 'Unchristian education is the source of hatred between nations.'[32] He also used to say that Europeans seemed like barbarians in comparison to Americans. The form of this phrase is paradoxical, however its content is significant and relates not only to technical development and the societal system, but also to the dignity and value of people's souls.

I only fully understood and evaluated the sentence I have quoted from my late father's work once I had come to know America.

* * *

The siren wails and the ship slides majestically out of the dock. On the balconies the multicoloured, densely packed crowds bid the travellers farewell with a mighty cheer. This must be the reverberation of human hearts since it rises so high above all else. Like swarms of butterflies colourful banners on the ship and on the shore flutter towards each other; small American flags are predominant, some being taken away by the travellers, some waved in farewell by those staying under the great Star-Spangled Banner. Americans know how to treasure and love their national flag and are not ashamed to show it.[ii] They have carved out a large chunk of the world's land, a large chunk of the world's heavens and established dominion over it, scattering it with stars, which, although each possesses its own independent rotation and direction, are subject to shared, unassailable laws while mutual gravitational forces maintain their cosmic system. So together they forge ahead along harmonious routes into the endless distance — towards their suns.

This corner of clear and starry sky lies on the great flag of the world where heart's blood and truth are alternately displayed; ever more new suns are entering this interdependent system and so one day the whole banner of humankind will stop running with blood and all of the human race will strive for the stars — '*ad astra!*'

America, with its anthill of human labour, the epitome of dignity and order, with its green shore dotted with neat, little houses, recedes into the distance.

---

ii The national flag of the United States of America displays alternating white and red fields. In one corner there is a blue field strewn with stars. There are as many stars as there are States. There were 13 when independence was declared; the number continues to increase; currently there are 48.

On the last island the enormous figure of the Statue of Liberty is outlined against the sky. Rays around her forehead, she bids us farewell with her arm raised powerfully upwards; in her other hand a book of laws, salvation from the bondage of evil. In her raised hand she holds a torch: the light of freedom, a Promethean spark. She bids us farewell, she summons us, she cautions us. She addresses us using the words of the great historiosophist von Rotteck from over a century ago, 'If reactionary forces prevail, then nothing will be able to stop the backward slide and Asia will be the mirror in which we see our future fate. Then — as once in the declining Byzantine Empire — there will be no enjoyment of life nor reward for the toils of daily existence for souls which are noble and proud. It is true that freedom will not disappear from the world, but Europe will only see that holy fire shine from beyond the Atlantic.'[33]

* * *

I recorded my impressions of America in letters to my family during my trips in 1910 and 1912. I compiled those notes into this account in Kraków in 1916.

I know I will face accusations of a rose-tinted outlook and bias in describing the situation in America, and that people will listen with incredulity hearing about the standard of living actually in place in America as it is beyond our wildest dreams, an unattainable ideal. A few years have passed since I visited America, so I have had time to digest my impressions and reinforce them in practical ways. I have had the opportunity to verify my views in numerous conversations with people who know the United States well. All these factors have entrenched my impressions, turning them into convictions.

American civilisation is the expression of the unfettered Aryan spirit: individualistic, freedom-loving, but with a sense of order; clear-headed, yet pushing tirelessly ahead — towards lofty ethical and humane ideals. After the current war the divergence in the future course of American and European history foreseen by perspicacious thinkers will become even more markedly pronounced than it has been till now. The material and moral disasters that will be visited on Europe by the present war will widen the gap between the civilisations of America and Europe.

140 years ago, at the time when the United States gained independence in the New World, in Europe an independent, freedom-loving state — the Polish-Lithuanian Commonwealth — was perishing. At the same time as the values of morality, freedom and respect for human dignity were serving as the foundations for a new social order in America, Europe, driven by arrogance, was breaking faith with its mission and knowingly supressing the instinct for truth and justice embedded in the consciences of individuals and humankind. This sin against the Holy Ghost has visited a sentence of damnation upon Europe; the present cataclysm is a consequence of that sin and a harbinger of the imminent and final extermination of European civilisation.

An Outline of the History of the United States[34]

The character of a nation, even though it may be subject to considerable deviation within a particular generation, leaves a distinct mark on its history. Familiarising ourselves with an outline of the historical development of the United States gives us a key to improving our understanding of the essential character of Americans: they themselves cherish and take pride in their past, assiduously preserving their own heritage. They live by the lofty ideals contained in their Constitution, ideals that led them to fight for independence, for the abolition of slavery and for the dignity of their nation. With great reverence they nurture the spiritual legacy of their great statesmen — great men indeed! It was these men's moral stature that raised them to positions of leadership and left their imprint on the spiritual evolution of the American nation.

A short outline of the history of the United States should throw light on many current phenomena in which the character of Americans plays a role. It will link the past and the present and allow us to draw conclusions about the future.

* * *

Attempts to colonize North America by the English, the Spanish, the French and the Dutch started in the XVII Century. By the end of that century, wars were breaking out between the English and French colonies. The causes lay both in animosities rooted in Europe and in local disagreements, and religious differences were also a contributing factor. There were four of these wars within a period of 60 years; each war lasted a number of years. Both sides used various Indian tribes as reinforcements. The last of these wars continued for 10 years, eventually ending in 1763 with France finally defeated. During this war George Washington, who was later to become the first President of the United States, distinguished himself in battle.

As the long-running wars between the English and French settlers ended and receded into the background, the question of England's relationship to its colonies on the Atlantic Ocean came to the fore. There were 14 of these colonies and each was a separate administrative entity and had established its own laws equivalent to a constitution, however these laws were violated when it suited the interests of those in power. Some colonies had been granted to English peers. The colonies were ruled by governors sent over from England who concentrated on looking after the interests of the mother country, and to an even greater extent, their own interests; they oppressed the local populace in a shameful way, imposing ever greater restrictions on its political rights and autonomy. As early as the second half of the XVII Century this led to armed resistance. England was exploiting its colonies economically and not giving them anything in return. The English Parliament introduced a monopoly on all the American colonies' imports and exports for the benefit of the mother country. Colonies were not even allowed to transport their own finished products between themselves; this included e.g. hats, which were an important sector of the domestic economy. All independent development in the colonies was suppressed. Moreover, England decided to impose taxes on the colonies for the benefit of the English Treasury without giving anything to the colonies in return, not even an effective right to local self-government, let alone seats in Parliament. In pursuit of this taxation policy, in 1765 the English authorities enacted a law which made it compulsory to use British stamped paper for all legal documents, bills, newspaper publications etc. The entire population of America saw this as yet another attack and resisted so resolutely, using the slogan 'no taxation without representation', that the British government had to repeal the Stamp Act. However, as the British government wanted to uphold the principle of its right to tax the colonies and maintain a monopoly on trade, it introduced a tax on tea. The rules for calculating this tax were intentionally set up to make English tea cheaper than the tea that other countries could supply, after taxation had been taken into account. But precisely because there was a principle at stake, all the people resisted and in protest, threw tea supplies on British ships overboard. The English Parliament responded with repressive measures.

The winds of freedom and radical change swept through wide swathes of the country. Colonies started establishing their own militias. Patrick Henry, a statesman from the Colony of Virginia memorably articulated the prevailing sentiment, 'Is life so dear or peace so sweet as to be purchased at the price of chains and slavery? Forbid it, Almighty God! I know not what course others may take; but as for me, give me liberty or give me death!'[35]

Previous jealousies between the colonies receded as a result of these events; they were now united by a common purpose. As a consequence of the infamous Stamp Act, representatives of nine colonies met in New York. Several years later in 1774 a congress gathered in Philadelphia, which in fact was only a convention of delegates from 13 colonies. It had moral authority only, but this was the first tiny seed that would in future grow into the great federation of the United States. The Congress sent a petition to the King and Parliament asking for reinstatement of the colonies' rights to self-government. In the meantime, the colonies began to assemble military forces. On 18th April 1775 a British general in Boston sent his troops to seize the military stores of the militia in the local area. That led to the Battle of Lexington, the first battle between the English army and the colonial militia. It ignited a revolution which blazed in colonies throughout the whole country from north to south. The Continental Congress, which was still gathered in Philadelphia, appointed George Washington as the Commanding General. The early stages of this military action could be characterised as a rebellion of British citizens fighting for their rights, but in time the policies pursued by the English government made it clear that the colonies had to make independence their goal. On 4th July 1776 the Continental Congress approved the renowned Declaration of Independence in which the term United States of America was used for the first time and all ties of dependence with Great Britain were thereby ceremoniously severed. This legal instrument ends with the words, 'And for the support of this Declaration, with a firm reliance on the protection of Divine Providence, we mutually pledge to each other our Lives, our Fortunes, and our sacred Honor.'[36] Adams and Jefferson, the principal authors of this momentous founding proclamation, both later served as President and both died on 4th July 1826 on the 50th anniversary of the Declaration of Independence. The bitter war lasted for years, with twists and turns in the fortunes of the two sides, and the American armies frequently found themselves in a hopeless situation. This battle for freedom aroused growing sympathy in Europe and volunteers from Europe started to arrive in America. Among them were the outstanding young Marquis de Lafayette; the champion of freedom and order, Kościuszko; Pułaski, who died in the Battle of Savannah in Georgia in 1778; and several distinguished German officers. The tenacity of the Americans, the increasing circulation in France of American-influenced slogans about freedom and lastly French envy of England led to France signing a treaty with the United States in early 1778. This treaty significantly improved the situation of the American armies as the English now feared a blockade by the French fleet. Despite this the war continued until 1782 (seven years all in all) when England, after suffering yet another defeat, realised that even substantial military victories would never suffice to keep the colonies as vassal states; later England signed a peace treaty.

Once the peace treaty was signed, Washington, who was adored by the people, resigned from the post of Commanding General and retired to the privacy of his home on a farm in Mount Vernon, in the area where the city of Washington was later built.

The confederated States had a population of just under 4 million at that time. The States were linked together, but only very loosely. Congress did not even have the ability to raise taxes to pay for an army. The political system varied in each State. The States were entirely independent of each other. This separatism did not cease even during the war they fought together.

The Continental Congress acted as no more than an assembly point for the representatives of the independent states in the federation; it had very little authority. This had already had negative consequences during the war: even the most important initiatives proposed by Washington himself could not be implemented because of the lack of unity and the unwillingness of individual States to yield. However, the trials and tribulations of such a long war did have some unifying effect on the group of colonies. During the war a decision was eventually made, although there were difficulties and resistance in reaching it, that each State should only have one vote in Congress even if it had delegated several representatives. The Congress did finally manage to formalise its own rules towards the end of the war in 1781, but as a result of its impotence, its standing was low both at home and abroad. It was evident that a lack of a strong government would lead the country to ruin. Five years after the peace with England had been agreed, this led the people of all the States to summon a new convention in Philadelphia for the purpose of creating a shared constitution to permanently unite the individual States and so empower the nation. George Washington was called away from the private life he had been leading to preside over this convention. It was an extremely difficult task to persuade the delegates to drop their separatist, petty interests and animosities and create a strong central government. Several delegates withdrew; all the creative work that had been done so far was at risk of falling apart. Wise statesmen who loved their country feared for its future. Benjamin Franklin,[iii] [37] a venerable and respected statesman, despaired at the turn talks were taking and suggested that, since human reasoning had been exhausted and the only hope lay in God, they start all remaining sessions of the convention with prayers. In the end they came to an agreement, contentious issues were resolved, and they unanimously recommended acceptance of the Constitution, which consequently, in stages and with difficulty, was adopted by all the States within a period of a few years. The individual States did not want to renounce their sovereignty; they had reservations about recognising a superior, shared government; some had reservations about the role of President of the United States, seeing parallels with the power of a monarch.

The Constitution adopted at that time has survived to the current day with only minor changes.

In 1789, Washington, who was revered by all, was chosen as the first President of the United States. After the four-year term specified by the Constitution had passed, he was re-elected unanimously despite the continued existence of rumps of the old federalist and anti-federalist factions. The anti-federalist faction did include a number of decent men, patriots who feared government by the President and Congress might become comparable to the rule of the English King and Parliament, a regime they had just overturned. Despite this the

iii Benjamin Franklin was the son of a chandler, himself a printer, then a publisher, later Postmaster General, a scholar who discovered the electric charge in clouds and invented the lightning conductor, compassionate and active on behalf of the community, a politician, and one of the authors of the Declaration of Independence. An ambassador to France at the time of the war, he helped negotiate the peace treaty with England. It was said of him, 'He snatched lightning from the sky and the scepter from tyrants.'

leaders of both parties had taken a seat in the same Cabinet — the first Cabinet of the United States.

When his second term as President expired Washington refused to accept a further nomination and settled down on his farm again.

John Adams was chosen as the next President after Washington: he was a representative of the Federalist Party i.e. the political party with a conservative bent which wanted strong central government. But he was succeeded by Jefferson, the leader of the Democratic-Republican Party, a man who was his opponent politically, although they had worked together in the same Cabinet and also on the task of creating the Constitution.

The momentous achievement of gaining independence and establishing a permanent framework for a new nation state without any violent internal upsets can be attributed to the high moral qualities of the populace and the righteous character of the statesmen who led it.

After the United States gained independence, the previous social order based on government nominations and privileges for certain social classes started to give way to a more democratic tendency, which guaranteed personal freedom for all and the opportunity to move up in society in line with one's capabilities and moral qualities.

The Constitution in its original form did not eliminate Negro slavery, but in some States the position of slaves was made less onerous. At that time only one State, Massachusetts, treated slavery as unlawful. That stance was also taken by Jefferson, one of Kościuszko's friends, who later became President of the United States. A law enacted in 1787 determined that Negro slavery could continue in the southern States, but prohibited it in the northern States and the territories lying to the north of the river Ohio. That is why those States were known as "free States". In 1808 importation of new slaves from abroad was prohibited in all States.

A few years after the peace treaty was signed, another war with England almost broke out. England had kept its military forts among the American Indian tribes in the territories to the west of the 13 confederated States and resisted passing them over to the Americans. Indeed, to strengthen its own hand it stirred up the American Indian tribes against the Americans. This led to many long years of ongoing battles with the American Indians. In the end England agreed to hand over these territories to the United States a year after the peace treaty.

During the war between France and England which started in 1793, Americans, who were generally sympathetic to the French Revolution and grateful to France for its support during the American War of Independence, wanted to declare war against England. The party of the so-called "democrats", in other words the anti-federalists, pushed particularly hard for this to happen. President Washington and the federalists tried to maintain neutrality; this was difficult because of pressure from France, pressure from England, and also because of domestic friction. Those who supported neutrality were known as Anglophiles and the "democrats" as Francophiles. The battles over maintaining neutrality lasted seven years. During this period, to prove its neutrality the American government sent a representative to England to negotiate a treaty of amity and commerce, much like the one that existed with France, and in the course of these negotiations the matter of the disputed territories mentioned earlier was resolved. These diplomatic moves infuriated the

Francophiles. Despite the attempt to maintain neutrality, a war with France was only just avoided. The Directorate was angered by the United States agreeing a treaty with England and broke off diplomatic relations. It then insulted the American commission sent to France to preserve peace by demanding a loan from America and threatening war if the loan was not forthcoming.

The affection which freedom-loving America had hitherto felt for republican France changed overnight into feelings of injured pride and outrage at France's behaviour. The call was, 'Millions for defense, but not one cent for tribute.'[38] Napoleon did not want to be at war with America so he agreed a convention with the United States.

The north-western territories up to the river Mississippi belonged to the United States. Beyond the Mississippi the whole of the enormous central area right up to the Rocky Mountains, which was called Louisiana, belonged originally to Spain and then, under Napoleon I, to France. Aware that he would not manage to keep this land, in particular the New Orleans port at the mouth of the Mississippi which was the sole object of interest for the Americans, Napoleon offered delegates from the United States the purchase of the whole of this enormous territory for a sum of 15 million dollars — a proposal which the delegation accepted on their own authority. In this way the United States gained lands substantially larger than those they had possessed up till then.

The war between England and France and their reciprocal blockades caused frequent altercations with the United States, whose ships were attacked by both warring countries. This led to the War of 1812 between the United States and England. The insubstantial American fleet managed to gain some victories over the mighty English fleet due to the Americans' tremendous daring and vigour. There were some temporary defeats, but in battles on the Canadian border and in the south, through sheer valour the Americans managed to demonstrate their strength to the English; the result was the peace agreed in a treaty in December 1814 without any concessions on either side.

In the period from 1815 onwards the United States occupied itself with domestic affairs. President Monroe's period of office (1817–1825) was known as the Era of Good Feelings. The federation expanded as new States were gradually accepted into the Union. Increasingly large numbers of immigrants were being attracted to the United States by factors such as the rate of economic development, the feeling of respect for American valour prevailing in Europe, the return of peace and stability, and most important of all the political freedom prevailing in America at a time when reactionary forces prevailed in Europe following the shameful Congress of Vienna. The following table shows the growth in immigration.

Immigration to the United States

In the decade	1811–1820	114	thousand
	1821–1830	143	"
	1831–1840	600	"
	1841–1850	1,700	"
	1851–1860	2,600	"
	1861–1870	2,500	"
	1871–1880	2,900	"
	1881–1890	5,200	"
	1891–1900	3,800	"
	1901–1910	8,700	"

Substantial advances in the means of transport, a matter of the utmost importance in the virgin lands of such an enormous continent, contributed to the progress in colonizing and developing the country. In 1807 Fulton launched his first steamboat on the river Hudson. The first railway line was built in 1830 and immediately afterwards more and more new lines began to be constructed at an extraordinary speed. In 1835 Morse invented the electrical telegraph, although it took nine more years for Congress to erect the first telegraph line which ran between Washington and Baltimore.

The following examples serve to illustrate the scale of development in the United States in that period: in 1830 there were 30 miles of railway track in the whole country, but by 1840 there were 3,000 miles. The central States on the shores of the Great Lakes — the western part of the country at the time — doubled their population in that decade, and some States even experienced a fivefold increase. It was in this period that Chicago became a city. In 1838 steamships started making regular voyages across the Atlantic Ocean. In 1855 the Union paid off all its debts and became the only country to be debt-free. A strange sequence of events led to a dreadful financial crash and economic recession only two years later. The crash was caused by fevered speculation, banks in each State issuing banknotes (the money of the national bank, i.e. the Union's bank, had been divided up between these State banks), and the government's budget surpluses. These surpluses arose because the national bank had been shut down in 1833 due to a doctrinaire approach among the political groupings influencing the government of the day. The attrition of moral standards in politics was also a contributing factor.

Aspiring to form independent republics as the United States had done, the Spanish colonies to the south of the United States broke away from Spain in 1821 and formed the Mexican Republic. In America there were fears that the European states would assist Spain in subjugating its colonies. In his address to Congress on the 2nd December 1823, the incumbent president, Monroe, announced the principle, henceforth known as the Monroe Doctrine, that the United States would oppose any attempt by European powers 'to extend their system or interfere in any portion of America'.[39] This was a declaration that the principle of independence applied to the whole of the New World and it was also a challenge to the Holy Alliance of the Congress of Vienna. The Monroe Doctrine also recognised the principle of American non-intervention in European affairs.

Around 1830 tensions heightened over the long-standing issue of the sovereignty of individual States versus the power of Congress and central government. These forerunners of the secessionists defended their right to interpret the Constitution in their own fashion: they saw it as an arrangement between sovereign states with an implicit right to nullification of resolutions passed by Congress and the government. The most prominent ringleader in this destructive movement was Calhoun from South Carolina. Supporters of federalism opposed this tendency. One of their leaders — Webster from Massachusetts — was an equally powerful orator. He defended the principle that the Constitution of the Union was not just an arrangement between sovereign states, claiming that the people of the United States had created a strong central administration which had the authority to implement its statutes. President

Jackson supported this interpretation which was aligned with the principles he had formulated thus, 'Our Union must be preserved. The laws of the United States must be executed. The object of those who espouse the right to nullification is disunion and disunion, by armed force, is treason.'[40]

The disputes between these two factions continued but did not lead to any violent confrontations.

However, the differences relating to slavery were becoming increasingly pronounced; it was recognised by law in some States and considered unlawful in others. In the south, i.e. in the States with plantation owners dependent on slave labour, they even postulated a theory that the only natural relationship conducive to social harmony when two races met was one of master and slave and hence their social order was legitimate. We see this principle of *des herrscher-volkes* [ruling people] ruling over *minderwertige Nationalitäten* [inferior nationalities] in Germany and in the Prussian Junker class at the beginning of the XX Century. In essence this matter could not be resolved by the federal constitution because the central government was unable to impose a solution due to the fact that since the beginning of the XIX Century half of the States represented in Congress were "free States" i.e. ones that did not allow slavery, while the other half upheld the institution. This was also the reason that both sides were wary of the opposing side gaining a majority when new States were accepted into the Union, and so new States were, in effect, admitted in pairs. In 1820 Missouri asked to be admitted to the Union while keeping the right to preserve the institution of slavery. Congress debated Missouri's request for Statehood for three sessions and finally agreed on a compromise: Missouri would be accepted into the

Union, however slavery would be prohibited forever in all territories to the north and west of the State of Missouri.

Many colonists from the United States settled on land which was part of Mexican Texas. In 1835 a rebellion erupted in response to oppression by the Mexican government and Texas declared itself an independent republic. Ten years later Texas demanded to join the Union. This was agreed but only after lengthy negotiations since Texas's laws permitted slavery and once again the same issue recurred. Texas's admission to the Union led to a drawn-out war with Mexico which refused to relinquish its claims to its former colony. Peace was not agreed until 1848 after its capital — Mexico City — had been captured. Under the terms of the peace treaty the United States relinquished its demands for compensation for losses suffered by United States citizens prior to the war while for its part Mexico ceded to the United States the vast, barren and virtually uninhabited areas of land which stretched from just west of the Rocky Mountains right up to the Pacific Ocean. In a further arrangement the United States paid Mexico a sum of 15 million dollars. After the Americans (let's use that term to refer to all citizens of the United States) annexed this territory, known at the time as the Great Californian Desert, migration to those lands of the distant Wild West commenced. It intensified after immense gold deposits were discovered in California within a year of the peace accord.

At first savage relations prevailed amongst the buccaneers chasing gold and adventure. Even in this situation Americans demonstrated their incredible aptitude for self-government and their ability to combine individual freedom with respect for the rule of law: on their own initiative they established order, passed a constitution (which prohibited slavery) and made a formal request to Congress for admission to the Union, all within a year of the mass influx of emigrants.

The development of this enormous agglomeration which stretched from the Atlantic to the Pacific and was equal in size to Europe (including the European part of Russia) was aided by an abundance of metals of all kinds, the cattle in Texas, and the ease of communication along the long coastline of the Pacific Ocean. The addition of Texas and, to its west, the Territory of New Mexico and the "free State" of California, once more raised the contentious issue of slavery. It had not been debated in Congress since the Missouri Compromise of 1820 in order to avoid stirring up animosities between the two groups of States. Once broached, the subject reignited passionate debate once more. The southern slave-holding States demanded the surrender of Negro fugitives who had escaped to the "free States". The people of the northern States would not agree to this. In 1852 Henrietta Beecher-Stowe's world-renowned novel *Uncle Tom's Cabin* was published, which spoke out on behalf of the slaves. Few books have had such enormous impact: it inflamed public opinion, already long opposed to slavery, and its eventual consequence was the terrible war over the abolition of slavery. The struggle struck a chord in Europe as it dealt with the fundamental issues of freedom and human rights. For this reason, in Russia for example *Uncle Tom's Cabin* was banned until 1860.

The southern States were aggrieved by the fierce condemnation of their stance on slavery and they were not spared, even in Congress. Slavery harmed the work prospects of "poor Whites" and the development of industry in the southern States. In 1854 violent altercations started over the issue of slavery in connection with the admission to statehood of Nebraska and Kansas. Both the supporters of slavery and their opponents wanted to populate these Territories in order that their own standpoint would prevail. This led to bloody clashes.

Slavery was the main focus of the campaigns in the presidential election of 1856. Indeed, there were predictions circulating that the matter would lead to secession since there was no possibility of settling it in a conciliatory manner. It was also not helpful that the Supreme Court (from which there was no right of appeal) was asked to rule on matters relating to slavery. The population of the northern States feared that a decision by the Supreme Court might give the citizens of the "slave States" the right to hold slaves and to seek out fugitive slaves in the "free States". On the other hand, the southerners were outraged that in 1859 in the hills of Virginia a small group of a dozen or so abolitionists had started to free slaves using force. The leader of this gang was caught and executed, but the southerners feared that such antics by the abolitionists might precipitate mass rebellion by the Negroes. Meanwhile new "free States" were accepted into the Union which gave the "free States" a majority in Congress. In 1860 in a period of extremely heightened tensions Abraham Lincoln[iv] was elected President. Seven of the

---

iv Lincoln, the son of poor squatters who settled in the wild Indiana Territory, was a self-made man, a type common in America. Franklin, Grant and others also belonged to this category. Lincoln grew up in very tough circumstances. He was self-taught and had difficulty acquiring an education in the rough circumstances of his upbringing. In his youth he was a farmhand, then he worked transporting goods on the Mississippi, subsequently he worked as a shop assistant, then a land surveyor, eventually he studied law and became a politician valued for his abilities and his probity; finally he became a Congressman and then President at a time when the country was in grave crisis. By the end even the southerners valued his wisdom and fairness.

southern States demanded the dissolution of their bond to the Union; they declared independence as secessionists at the start of 1861. The northern States called a peace conference to look for a compromise, but the southerners did not attend; instead they formed a government for the new Confederate States of America with its seat in Richmond and elected a President. All attempts to temper the conflict were unsuccessful. Widespread turmoil ensued. Many people in the southern States did not want to leave the Union; in the northern States some held the view that the southern States could not be kept in the Union by force, while others treated the events as a clear case of rebellion against the Constitution. The President maintained a neutral position.

It was not just the question of slavery that caused the war: it was also the matter of how the fundamental function of the Union was interpreted. One side claimed, 'Our States are sovereign and have the right to leave the Union if they believe they have cause to do so.' The other side said, 'You are part of a Union which brings into being a single nation and fracturing that Union equates to rebellion.' Passions were stirred to the utmost. The decision about war or peace was no longer in the hands of the President or Congress. The fighting erupted spontaneously. The Confederates bombarded a port garrisoned by the United States. Four more southern States joined the Confederates i.e. the secessionists. In the northern States 100,000 volunteers enlisted in the army within three days and enormous sums were donated to finance the war. In the southern States they also took up arms with fervour and determination. A tempestuous civil war had been unleashed, however no-one anticipated how burdensome, long and bloody that war would be. The Americans' innate doggedness and valour meant that neither side could vanquish the other. This harrowing conflict lasted four years. There were 2,400 battles fought. The fact that in the battle of Gettysburg both armies lost almost a third of their men, altogether 48,000 people, serves as a measure of the fervour with which they fought — and this was not an isolated incident. Approximately one million people perished in this war. The cost of the war on the northern States' side was 3½ billion dollars, which even in today's terms is an enormous sum. The depletion and devastation of the country were so great that comparisons were drawn with the havoc wreaked by the Thirty Years' War; however the latter did not yield much in the way of positive outcomes whereas the American Civil War secured the triumph of the principles for which the "free States" fought.

At the start of April 1865 General-in-Chief Lee capitulated on behalf of the last remaining army of the southern States. The Commanding General of the northern States' army General Ulysses Grant together with his staff treated the defeated side with respect and exemplary courtesy. The only conditions for peace were the abandonment of all hostilities and the surrender of all the southern army's weapons. They were allowed to keep their horses as 'You'll need them for ploughing as it's spring now.'[41] In essence this fundamental issue had been resolved in favour of the northern States' ideals. The Union and slavery could not coexist. The victory of the northern States preserved the Union and slavery was abolished. Ideals had won the day. No-one thought to grind down or exploit the southern States, quite the opposite: they started to even out the differences which had divided the two warring camps for so many years and then in the end pushed them into the abyss of the most horrific war. Even the assassination of the revered President Lincoln by a southern fanatic a few days after the surrender of the southern army did not hinder reconciliation between the former enemies. Naturally the party which had previously demanded to keep the institution of slavery lost its influence in Congress and in the government.

The peoples of Europe cheered on the northern States during the American Civil War, whereas the governments — concealed their joy at America's enfeeblement. During the civil war both sides resorted to issuing a substantial quantity of banknotes, which led to depreciation in their value and an ostensible rise in prices. The drop in the currency's value had a particularly adverse impact on the Confederated Southern States whose ports were subject to a blockade designed to prevent goods, weapons in particular, being delivered from Europe and exchanged for cotton. After the war banknotes issued by the southern States lost all their value. It is typical of America that in the course of the civil war no-one was sentenced to death for their political convictions. Even the secessionists' president, Davis, who was accused of high treason, was released after two years' internment. In 1862 during the war, President Lincoln, as the commander-in-chief of the armed forces, had issued a proclamation emancipating Negroes. After the war's end the Constitution was amended to abolish slavery throughout all the States and Territories of the United States. In 1870 Negroes were given citizenship rights. This was somewhat premature and thus made progress towards better relations between the White and Negro races more difficult. For some years after the war had ended slavery continued to provoke conflict between the southern and northern States. Reforms had to be implemented in the south. This did not always proceed smoothly, and naturally caused discontent amongst those who had been deprived of their voting rights for participating in the rebellion. In some States granting equal rights to the Negroes led, in reality, to their subjugation. In the end supremacy of Whites over Blacks in the southern States was brought about without any resistance from the Negroes — a passive race, in reality an inferior race which did not even engage in the battles for its own emancipation, although there were 3½ million slaves to 5½ million Whites in the southern States at the time. Both north and south worked together on the reconstruction of the southern States as their economy had been devastated by the war and by the abolition of slavery. Previously the economy of the south had been based on cotton and sugar cane cultivation using slave labour, but it was now undergoing a fundamental shift towards industry and commerce, following the template provided by the north. Despite all the upheavals agriculture clearly continued to be an important sector since the natural environment favoured it.

The secessionist States had to be rehabilitated and formally re-admitted to the Union by Congress. Within six years of the end of the war all the disputes and arguments were finally settled. Within a dozen or so, all that remained of the previous conflicts and hatred were recollections; peaceful political coexistence was the order of the day.

It would be inaccurate to say economic rivalry between the two groups of States was the hidden cause of the war. Their economic and social frameworks differed significantly: industry, commerce and a more democratic outlook were dominant in the north while the south tended towards an agrarian feudal system. In agriculture there was no cause for economic rivalry as they produced totally different crops. The northern States did not have any economic stake in the decision about which system prevailed in the south; for them the central issue was slavery and the other key issues were preserving the Union as a federal state and national unity. In contrast the southerners actually did have an economic interest in maintaining the institution of slavery since its abolition signified financial ruin. Because little credence could be given to the purity of intention of any person claiming slavery was justified, the principle virtually always invoked when the real issue was slavery was the right not to recognise the supremacy of federal law, at its extreme the right to break away from the Union.

From 1862 until 1876 there were ongoing battles with American Indians who kept attacking settlers in the central and western States. It was impossible for two races to coexist where one was nomadic and survived by hunting and raiding, while the other settled in one place and cultivated the land; one lived off land communally owned by its tribe, the other recognised private ownership of farmlands; one lived in a primitive state without any civilising influences or progress, the other was developing vigorously. The tribes were incapable of adapting to new conditions and could not survive the onward rush of civilisation. Even the federal laws enacted to protect the American Indians could not prevent the race's gradual decline.

In 1867 the United States enlarged its territory by purchasing Alaska from Russia for a sum of 7 million dollars, even though Alaska was of no benefit at the time. It did not take long for American enterprise to bring to light the immeasurable treasures which could be extracted from the ground in Alaska.

Substantial advances were being made in industry, trade and agriculture in the free and law-abiding United States. Important technological inventions supported this progress: machinery used in industry and agriculture (including a machine which separated cotton seeds from the fibres so making practicable cotton production on a massive scale), the telephone, the typewriter and thousands of improvements in industry, construction, the railways etc. In 1869 the construction of the first transcontinental railway was completed, linking the Atlantic and the Pacific. This really opened up the Far West. Cereal crop production on these great expanses of land (before most of them were later divided up into smaller farms) was managed as a large-scale capitalist industry as if in a factory, and the grain flooded into Europe. At the same time industry, mining and commerce were all developing. Extremely rapid economic development triggered frequent economic crises. These in turn encouraged the formation of trusts (subject to strict legal restrictions) and associations of small-scale farmers on the one hand, and on the other — gave rise to strikes and the formation of trade unions. The ever-increasing number of European immigrants heightened tensions over employment relations. Despite this, farmers' parties, workers' parties, and to an even greater extent the internationalist and revolutionary movements, all failed to find fertile ground for expansion in America. The principle of sovereignty of the people, consistently implemented, made it possible to satisfy the needs of various groups in society in a peaceful manner. Socialism, which was introduced mainly by German immigrants, did not suit the free and individualistic American spirit, while Americans' sense of order, respect for the law, and the strong government prevented any untoward incidents; the populace also assisted by tolerating theoretical ramblings but energetically dealing with any irregular behaviour.

In the second half of the XIX Century the United States continued to steer clear of world politics and battles between nation states. Attention was focused mainly on domestic economic policies: public finances, the currency and tariffs. Public finances and the currency (paper banknotes following the Civil War) were soon put in order, but the policies on tariffs were the subject of continual disputes between the interested parties and often led to serious problems related to the country's budget surplus. Squabbling between parties (not really related to ideology) and political pressure led to an extremely high level of corruption in official bodies, in which the Irish played a leading role. In 1883 a Civil Service Act was passed and a series of reforms were implemented which contributed substantially to making these relations healthy once more.

In the course of the 1876 elections a curious situation occurred which showed the political sophistication of Americans: due to procedural challenges to the electoral process in three States, it was not possible to decide which of two presidential candidates had won the elections. The Constitution did not provide any guidance for this situation. It caused a great deal of controversy. A committee of 15 members was chosen and it decided in favour of Hayes by a margin of one vote, although in fact his opponent had been selected in the election. However, the nation accepted, without any resistance, the verdict of the appointed committee and the president did not experience any difficulties in relation to this at any point during his period of office.

The Monroe Doctrine acted as a political signpost for the United States, guiding it to prioritise participation in matters most relevant to it: the colony of San Domingo, Cuba and the issue of the Panama Canal. Consequently, its long-term aim was closer economic and political co-operation between North, Central and South America. This presented enormous difficulties since the countries of these regions were separated by dissimilarities in cultural conditions and language, and hence in their needs and aspirations. The countries in the south feared the dominance of the United States and even aspired to create a union of South American, Romance-language-speaking countries as a counterbalance to the United States. The political unification of South America could have turned against other parts of the world, together with the United States, or it could have turned against the United States. For these reasons Pan-American congresses were difficult to organise, or they gathered but were incomplete, and those which did take place did not manage to achieve any significant results.

During the Cuban uprising against Spain in 1868–1878 Congress expressed support for Cuba and declared its readiness to accept Cuba into the Union, however the executive did not take any steps to make this happen. In this period the government of the United States warned European countries against ceding to each other any of their colonies on the American continent.

England, France and the United States all showed a keen interest in the Panama Canal project. The proposal for an international guarantee of the canal's neutrality did not satisfy the United States as it involved Europe in the affairs of the American continent. When France started building the Panama

Canal the United States began to seriously consider building a second, competing canal through Nicaragua. The bankruptcy of the company building the Panama Canal in 1889 simplified matters and the United States took on the completion of this momentous project.

Unprecedented and exceedingly rapid economic development triggered yet another recession towards the end of the XIX Century and consequently a period of intensified activity by trade unions and trusts at the beginning of the XX Century. The rate of immigration from Europe was still increasing (special rules had stemmed Asian immigration) which led to heightened tensions; moreover it threatened to dilute the Anglo-Saxon element, the people who really ran the country and were really the element of society of most value to the country. The state took action against the all-pervading rule of trusts by bringing very large industrial corporations of a public nature under its control.

Roosevelt, a great statesman and later the President, was very active in the anti-trust movement. He also took a vigorous approach to his role in the United States Civil Service Commission which had been set up previously. Its task was to reform and mend the ways in which official institutions operated, as these were disastrous at that time (around 1895), particularly in New York.

The question of tariffs clearly separated the Republican and Democratic parties: the former sought to fence off the American economy and for that reason they supported import duties, the latter pulled in the opposite direction. In 1897 President McKinley, a Republican, pushed through the introduction of high import tariffs, justifying this by the need to balance the national budget which had been in deficit for a few years and also by the need to bolster domestic industry. The previously planned income tax for the benefit of the federal treasury was highly unpopular and in the end was ruled unconstitutional by the United States Supreme Court on the basis that direct taxes were the domain of individual States. Introducing a strongly protectionist policy of high tariffs gave a remarkable boost to industrial development: American-manufactured goods produced using iron and textiles now significantly influenced world markets; as far as the public finances were concerned the national debt was reducing and in 1895 the United States started to deal on world financial markets as an investor seeking to place its capital. This was evidence that the development of the United States was, so to speak, complete and it was now acting as a country with an economy based on agricultural production and precious metals, but, in addition, with significant capability to export industrial goods. That was bound to trigger a search for markets for those goods in other countries.

In 1895 an uprising broke out in Cuba, which was caused principally by Spain's exploitative economic relationship with its colonies.

A strong faction of Creoles had been trying to cast off the Spanish yoke and form a political alliance with the United States since as early as 1840. Public opinion in the United States was very supportive of the insurrectionists' action so, in line with the Monroe Doctrine, the government decided to intervene and demanded the Spaniards withdraw from the island. Since diplomatic efforts came to nothing — they took military action.

The war ended very badly for Spain and it lost Cuba and also the islands of the Philippines to the United States.

In 1901 Cuba's freely elected parliament passed a constitution and presented the draft to the government of the United States for its approval. Cuba gained its independence with some restrictions relating to negotiating with foreign states about colonization and military matters. Thus the United States assumed no more than a protectorate over the new republic. In 1902 the Americans handed over power to the elected president and left the island.

The beginning of the XX Century was characterised by the exacerbation of existing socio-economic problems and this was the backdrop for the clashes between the Republicans and the Democrats. The Republican Party, which represented the interests of large-scale industry and the capitalists, sought to expand protectionism further, to introduce a grand style of colonial and imperialistic politics, and to tolerate a new type of immigration, namely the influx of cheap proletarian labour which was culturally low-ranking and linguistically distinct. The Democratic Party aimed to reduce the existing rates for customs duties, limit imperialistic policies and restrict immigration.

The recessions in the final decade of the last century were attributed to the Democratic governments and their tariff policy (President Cleveland's terms of office) which led to the Republicans taking over the helm of the country. However, their policies, like the current policies of the Democrats, were already to some extent the product of conflicting aspirations. Theodore Roosevelt (1901–1909), although a typical Republican, found himself forced to make certain concessions to the Democrats, mainly relating to controlling the ever more powerful trusts which had become the subject of vigorous protests by the general public.

His successor President Taft continued these policies. However after the Republican government introduced fresh rises in import duties in the 1909 Payne Tariff, public opinion turned against it. This was because through its tariff policy the government was seen to be facilitating the expansion of trusts in practice, despite fighting them by legislative means. The Democrats gained a large majority in Congress and in 1913 they succeeded in gaining the Presidency for their candidate Woodrow Wilson, a professor at Princeton University and the Governor of New Jersey.

Once in power however they also had to make certain concessions to the opposing party. So e.g. they now stand on a protectionist platform and limit themselves to mitigating its consequences. The imperialistic policies initiated by the Republicans, which took the form of expansion in the Pacific Ocean, Central and South America, were until recently categorically opposed by the Democratic Party, but they now continue under the Democrats and their government, admittedly in a measured and cautious way. An example of this was President Wilson's proposal to Congress to assume a protectorate over Nicaragua.

The Monroe Doctrine and Pan-American ideals play a significant role in this expansionism as they give the United States a basis for assuming protectorates over southern republics whose internal turmoil and financial disorder give due cause for it. This was the case when declaring a protectorate over San Domingo in 1904.

Besides Central America and South America, American expansionism is moving in another direction which has already been clearly mapped out, namely the Pacific Ocean. The United States has its own political and economic aims, but despite this it is conscious of its civilising mission and tries to fulfil it, mainly by sending numerous teachers and seconded staff to Asia. The United States managed to gain the trust of the countries of the Far East through its Open Door Policy and respecting those countries' territorial integrity. However, the waters of the Pacific Ocean conceal many potential problems that may trouble American politicians in the future.

The annexation of the Philippines sparked off conflict between the United States and Japan, which saw those islands as a natural complement to their own island state and ideal territory for colonization. The antagonism deepened over the issue of the Japanese immigrants who came to the United States (particularly in California) in large numbers at the beginning of this century. Relations became particularly strained after 1907 when a law was passed prohibiting any further immigration to California by the Japanese.

In the early years of this century American economic growth became an indomitable force which inevitably crossed its home country's borders, triggered by overproduction in its industries and in agriculture, which were both developing vigorously and expanding in scope. For this reason, for the first time we see some departure from the traditional principle of American politics encapsulated in Washington's testament and Monroe's doctrine — in essence the principle of not interfering in non-American affairs. Immense psychological strength is another factor contributing to American expansionism. This strength flows from Americans' belief in a new world order based on universal peace and respect for the law.

The combination of these material and spiritual strengths has shunted America onto new tracks in their life story — tracks which go beyond the borders of the American continent.

America and Europe Contrasted

All human pronouncements and predictions have failed us in the present war. Things have come to pass which go beyond human understanding and volition. The future course of events cannot be foreseen, not even in broad outline. And yet the human mind cannot restrain itself from reviewing past events which have led to the current cataclysm, nor from drawing conclusions about the future consequences of current events. It seems certain that we will not return to life in its previous form. Human emotions, and along with them thoughts, will no doubt flow in a different direction than they have until now.

Let's compare how concepts have evolved over the last 150 years in Europe and in America. The reaction to the tyranny and abuses of secular and religious authorities began in the XVIII Century. A powerful critic surfaced in Voltaire, but he lacked moral grounding; he vacillated between liberalism and adoration of that licentious woman — the tyrant Catharine II — and so his influence was exclusively destructive. Rousseau, a sentimentalist and near contemporary of Voltaire, absolved people of all fault in advance as he believed the causes of evil lay in people's environment, rather than in the choices they made. This pandered to those with weak and flimsy characters.

In the second half of the XVIII Century, atheism took hold in Europe. The French Revolution arrived and toppled everything; the idol it put forward was the paltry human intellect. The Revolution recognised the rights of man, but said nothing of his obligations, tasks or mission.

In this same period America was fighting for its liberty, but shaped by Puritan and other religious values, it based all its constitutions on the laws of morality, an imperative of a superior kind.

Napoleon I did not have any principles to depend upon so he raised the cry 'Fame and Honour!', insubstantial aspirations which yield too easily to personal interpretation.

In America at this time they were fighting to preserve their freshly gained independence. The history of the United States continued to show a process of development within the country, efforts to raise the cultural level of the nation, and finally great battles of principle to unite the country and abolish slavery. In Europe, following the fit of madness that was the French Revolution, the age of odious reactionary forces dawned and any outbursts of the free human spirit were quelled. The rulers of that world, devoid of any ethical sensibility, treated the interests of their dynasty or camarilla as their only guiding lights. In America the Gospel served as the basis for society's development and the government of the people, whereas in Europe it was the principles of Machiavelli, Metternich or Talleyrand. European statesmen treated ideals as a cloak which could help them achieve their selfish goals. The Byzantine rot was setting in.

At the same time in America, highly moral men were following in Washington and Franklin's footsteps, gaining esteem and influence with the nation.

From the time independence was declared in the United States until the present day, political development in America and Europe has followed fundamentally different paths. In Europe the interests of the state have dictated the character of the political system and the state's relationship to its **subjects**. Despite all the efforts of revolutionary movements, this system survived until the World War; the predominance of the state was increasing, quashing the rights of the individual as it grew. The current form of anarchism, known as Bolshevism, is a furious reaction against this.

In America at every point along the way the state has been subordinated to its **citizens**, who have bestowed on the state the power and duty to maintain law and order in society.

In the mid-XIX Century, philosophical naturalism and then materialism took hold in Europe; this led eventually to the acceptance of brute force as the sole deciding principle and of gratification as man's only goal. Revolutionary socialism emerged to defy the tyranny of governments and capitalism. It could have focused on improving the lot of the underprivileged classes, but preferred to pander to the lower instincts of the ignorant masses: it aroused hatred for the higher classes in society, a desire to grab power and a craving for gratification.

At the same time the Jews, liberated from the fetters restraining them until now, started their vengeful business of destabilising European society; they had already cut themselves off from it by creating an insurmountable barrier out of their hatred, their conceited egotism and their alien world view.

Under the influence of all these factors the population of Europe was increasingly discarding spiritual influences and drifting further and further towards utilitarianism, opportunism and spiritual anarchism. *'Was kaufe ich mir dafür?'* ['What's in it for me?'] became a byword in Europe; in America it was 'Go ahead!' and a desire to act.

Philosophical thought also followed different tracks: indifferentism and religious scepticism prevailed in Europe while in America a multitude of sects were developing, evidence that Americans were deeply involved in religious affairs and acknowledged human life had a higher purpose. Towards the end of the XIX Century even mysticism and practices using the power of the human will started to thrive in America.

In Europe moral laws, duty and God were supposed to function for man's benefit, rather than man serving them. Egotism had been superseded by ego worship.

This atmosphere bereft of ideals provided favourable conditions for the engorgement of tyranny. The governments ruled the states — the states ruled the nations; the states started to take over certain aspects of public life, so undermining human individuality. Although they have souls, people were relegated to functioning like machines, treated like human raw material, and sacrificed for the needs of the state. The state, or rather the governments, set the course in all aspects of public life and did it to suit their own needs, whatever those happened to be, and their own ideology.

Socialism adopted the same idea: it obliterated any individuality and undermined people's liberty. A system regimented like a factory or military barracks, which reduced all people to the same level, was supposed to make possible equal gratification for all.

The socialists promoted policies that would replace freelance work with state employment, and organise people's lives in line with directives and regulations drawn up at the whim of ministers by the oh-so-wise bureaucracy. These principles were trialled during the war when everything was nationalised, in other words collectivized, even a man's life and conscience.

They proposed remuneration dependent on the hours spent at work rather than the work completed; they argued that the work of a great, creative mind, with decades of preparation for its profession behind it, was of identical value to the physical labour of a mere youngster. This was a way of awarding a bonus for idleness and ignorance. They went even further with their intentions to diminish society's cultural level: they formulated the principle that when resolving the most complex political and social issues any illiterate or thief should have an equal say to a person with outstanding moral and intellectual qualities.

A fallacious interpretation of equality between people was taken to an absurd extreme, but it flattered the ignorant masses and the rabble. For the agitators flattery was the whole point: they were fully aware of what to think of this alleged equivalence between people. The worker whose role was mechanical, whose capacity for thought had lapsed, saw the world in terms of nuts and bolts, but a peasant knew full well that the apple saplings he planted and the horses he used in his work varied in quality. The dictators of the proletariat relied above all on the ignorant masses; in instances where false ideology was not effective, they stoked up greed and envy, they undermined respect for other people's property and incited the masses to covet property of their own. It was inevitable that anarchist ideology spread as a reaction to the abuses of power and the restrictions and humiliations visited upon individuals.

A European social system based on such premises could only lead to political and nationalistic banditry, which eventually infected relations between social classes, both at work and in their private lives. War between states was replaced by ongoing class warfare. Devoid of all ideals, humankind moved step by step towards a cataclysm. It started with a war declared in accordance with all the rules of clandestine diplomacy. The war was supposed to glorify dynastic rule, secure positions, wealth and power for the ruling elites, and benefit the states that had systematically laid the ground for it. The people would not have allowed war to break out, and that is precisely why they were given no say in the matter. They were faced with a fait accompli. The people were goaded, driven like slaves and sent to be slaughtered. The states which were invaded resisted heroically, but Europe was in danger of rule by the knout or by an iron fist. The latter party was winning the war. Then, America contributed new slogans, reviving ideals and the redeeming power of action.

Autocracy collapsed, as did its universe of false ideologies, but by then Europe's economy had been devastated, the cohorts of people at the most economically active stage of life had been wiped out and any remaining moral principles had been slashed at their roots. During the war the most appalling villainy, abominable behaviour and serious criminality not only proliferated in all spheres, but was sanctioned. People became inured to it during the war years and thought they were justified in applying the same methods and principles for their own ends after the war. A human herd had been let loose, to trample all before it.

The tenets of pillage, violence and despotism proclaimed by the previous rulers of the world were adopted by the most uneducated and the most uncouth strata of society. Any manifestation of culture was repulsive to them. Under the deluded slogan "dictatorship of the proletariat" power was seized by adept agitators who at best were indifferent to humankind, and at worst loathed it with a hatred worthy of the likes of Nero, Genghis Khan, Attila the Hun or Wilhelm II. It was not possible to reach a compromise with people acting in bad faith or those possessed by fake ideals or the savage rabble. When the worst instincts of the masses were aroused and violent emotions overriding all inhibitions unleashed, there was no option but the repressive measures essential to protect freedom and civilisation. The necessity of reactionary measures to counteract the reign of terror imposed by the rabble and its provocateurs became apparent. Once again power-hungry people would lead the populace to demonstrate that it had not matured enough to use its freedom wisely, that it must be treated like a herd of bulls. The ultimate battle for survival between a civilised, functioning society and the depths of savagery had to take place. Would that battle sap what remained of European society's vital forces? Would it not lead to a collapse into a state of lethargy in which European civilisation — certainly the civilisation of central and eastern Europe — would wither away, creating conditions in which a different civilisation, other races, would inevitably come to dominate this continent? We have seen the favourable historical and ideological conditions which prepared the ground for the rule of Bolshevism. Jews, who led the Bolshevik movement in Russia and championed it in Europe, appear to have played a peculiar and mysterious role in this process.

This role becomes easier to understand if you delve into the Jewish psyche. The Jews felt alien and despised in the countries where they lived so they were not bound by devotion to their country nor by any shared ideals held in common with Aryan nations; they were absorbed by the idea that they were "the chosen people" which would by rights dominate the world; they were taught by their religion and customs that any crimes against non-Jews were permissible; and hence they strove, with all the bitter determination and hatred that characterises them, to consciously and intentionally destroy Christian civilisation. They looked on with joy at the misfortunes, crimes and poverty befalling society, knowing that these reinforced the sway of the golden calf, understanding that, thanks to their own cunning, solidarity, detachment and the particular attribute they possess of flourishing within weak, decaying structures, they would be able to dominate in societies which were disorganised and damaged, both morally and physically. This is the way they planned to bring about the downfall and trampling of a race and culture they found loathsome; then "the chosen people" could rule over its ruins.

While Europe, under its despotic rulers, was gradually heading towards chaos and collapse, freedom-loving America ruthlessly stamped out all manifestations of anarchism coming to its shores from Europe. Socialism also developed differently in America; in that country, with its love of freedom and respect for individuality, socialism could not assume the shape it did in Europe with one class tyrannizing both individuals and society.

What impact the war will have on American society is a question yet to be answered. Will the Americans be infected by the venom of imperialism, or perhaps anarchy, through their contact with gangrenous Europe? Will the war leave its corrupting stain on them? One would assume that a society which has shown such readiness to act and such fortitude, which has managed to secure the freedom of mankind, will also, as a healthy organism with immunity, manage to fight off the germs transmitted from elsewhere. Moreover, it is possible the United States may isolate itself by applying some sort of quarantine to immigration from Europe, as in the current circumstances it may actually carry more risk than an influx of Chinese or Japanese people. America has saved Europe, but it cannot be Europe's nanny, nor its policeman. Roosevelt was right when he said that a man who has stumbled or fallen should be supported or helped to rise to his feet — but one should not walk for him nor continually hold him by the hand and lead him as he walks. Clearly Europe's future depends on its own strength and its own merits.

We are seeing the start of a savage battle over what is left of Europe's economic assets following the devastation wreaked by the war. Individuals, social classes and communities are tearing these assets out of each other's hands. Productive economic activity has become impossible in the midst of this all-pervasive plundering, hence the population is running down its remaining capital resources. As an inevitable result the battle for possessions and for the means to live has become even more ferocious. The people who manage to stay afloat are the ones who are the most brutal, the most cunning, have the least scruples when selecting means to an end and those most limited in their cultural needs. People at a more advanced intellectual and moral level will be shoved below the surface in accordance with the levelling policies of the socialists and of the grouping previously known as Russian nihilists, now called Bolsheviks. All that will remain of European civilisation will be no more, no less than **nothingness**... I cannot help but think of Stefan Buszczyński's prophetic words. In 1881 he wrote:

'Everyone is racing towards this **nothingness**: Teutonic and non-Teutonic nations, Tartars, Finns and Romance-language races; conservatives and radicals; some take an indirect path, others head straight for it! Aristocrats and democrats, steady people and volatile people, free people and the enslaved are all racing towards this **nothingness**! But which of you is not enslaved?! People push each other towards this **nothingness**; some in ignorance of what is happening, others fully aware. All foundations, all principles, all ties, everything has been destroyed! The catastrophe is inexorable! Fire! Fire! One can almost hear the snapping of timbers, the ominous rumbling! A few more years... maybe a dozen... or even quarter of a century... half at most... and your society will perish in flames or by drowning! Who knows how it will come about? Who knows by what means it will perish? But, perish it will! Yet no-one is raising the alarm! Yet no-one is calling for help! And your wise men are still seated with their arms firmly crossed!'[42]

So is there really no way out and no salvation for the population of Europe? There will be none for certain unless we see an extraordinary moral reversal in human souls, a mighty spiritual rebirth and an abundance of dedication and sacrifice. All humankind shares in this joint responsibility. A mountain of virtue is required to compensate for the mountain of evil;

the millions of criminals must be counterbalanced by at least thousands of saints... Is humankind capable of such a rebirth? Its future hangs on that question!

Endnotes

All quotations in this book have been translated by Kasia Beresford from the Polish versions presented by Buszczyński. In instances where the source quotation is in the English language the original wording has been inserted to the extent that Buszczyński's words are a plausible translation of it. As Buszczyński is very free in his approach to quotations there are omissions and additions, and he has at times paraphrased or made significant sequencing changes while still displaying the text within quotation marks. Major discrepancies are highlighted in the relevant endnotes.

1 These tenets are contained in a letter written by Stefan Buszczyński (the father of the author of this book) on the eve of his 60th birthday as his literary testament. The letter was included in a book published to celebrate his life and work: *Stefan Buszczyński i jego testament*, pp. 17–18, Drukarnia Związkowa pod zarządem A. Szyjewskiego, Kraków, 1892.

2 Theodore Roosevelt, 'Civic Helpfulness', published in the 'Century', October 1900. *The Works of Theodore Roosevelt*, Vol. 12 (of 14), pp. 96–7, P.F. Collier & Son, New York, 1901.

3 A term used by Theodore Roosevelt in his speech at the Hamilton Club in Chicago on 10 April 1899 and in his book *The Strenuous Life: Essays and Addresses* published the following year.

4 Wacław Sobieski, *Polska w Kulturze Powszechnej. Dzieło zbiorowe pod redakcyą Feliksa Konecznego Część I. Ogólna*, 'Kościuszko i Pułaski w Ameryce. (Zjednoczenie ideałów Polski i Ameryki).', p. 101, Polskie Spółki Oszczędności i Pożyczek, Kraków, 1918.

5 Ibid, pp. 90-1.

6 Appears to refer to a passage in van Dyke's book *The Spirit of America*, The Macmillan Company, 1912, where he talks about the American sense of humanity pp. 273–6 – 'In literature this feeling has shown itself in many ways. It has given a general tone of sympathy with "the under dog in a fight".'

7 In the original Polish text Buszczyński quotes this saying in English and provides a Polish translation which equates to: 'honesty is the best police'. The error may be a misprint or a misunderstanding or most likely an inadequate translation.

8 *Stefan Buszczyński i jego testament*, p. 19, Drukarnia Związkowa pod zarządem A. Szyjewskiego, Kraków, 1892, contains both this shortened version of the motto and the full version *'In voluntate unitas, in unitate libertas, in libertate salus'*.

9 The Constitution of Pennsylvania, 1776, § 10.

10 The Constitution of Delaware, 1776, art. 22.

11 The Constitution of South Carolina, 1778, art. 38, however this text refers to the requirements for establishment of a church, not a requirement for public office.

12 Abraham Lincoln, 'Gettysburg Address', Gettysburg, Pennsylvania, 19 November 1863.

13 The Constitution of the United States, 1789, pmbl. Buszczyński has joined two phrases which appear in the preamble, but do not follow directly one after the other.

14 Theodore Roosevelt, *American Ideals*, p. 20, G. P. Putnam's Sons, of New York and London, 1897.

15 Ibid, pp. 28-9.

16 Ibid, p. 22. Buszczyński has omitted the phrase 'in the last analysis' from the second sentence.

17 Ibid, p. 26. Buszczyński's Polish version of this quotation omits 'and resolute' from the phrase 'without an immediate and resolute effort' used in the original English.

18 Ibid, p. 26–7.

19 Ibid, p. 27. Buszczyński has omitted a few intervening sentences, so his version does not represent a continuous passage in the original.

20 Theodore Roosevelt, 'The Strenuous Life' speech, Hamilton Club, Chicago, 10 April 1899. *The Works of Theodore Roosevelt*, Vol. 12 (of 14), p. 4, P.F. Collier & Son, New York, 1901.

21 Ibid, p. 5. Buszczyński has omitted the phrase 'to keep himself, and to keep those dependent upon him.' at the end of the first sentence in the original.

22 Ibid, p. 6. Buszczyński has been very free in his manner of quoting here; in particular the second sentence appears to be a paraphrase of content from the original which appears before the first sentence.

23 Ibid, p. 21. Buszczyński has omitted part of the original sentence.

24 Theodore Roosevelt, 'Character and Success', published in the 'Outlook', 31 March 1900. *The Works of Theodore Roosevelt*, Vol. 12 (of 14), p. 98, P.F. Collier & Son, New York, 1901.

25 Theodore Roosevelt, 'The Eighth and Ninth Commandments in Politics', published in the 'Outlook', 12 May 1900. *The Works of Theodore Roosevelt*, Vol. 12 (of 14), p. 107, P.F. Collier & Son, New York, 1901. Buszcyzński has paraphrased here: in Roosevelt's original text the sentence ends with 'cardinal points in his doctrine ought to be "Thou shalt not steal," and "Thou shalt not bear false witness against thy neighbor".' (the Eighth and Ninth Commandments of the title) whereas Buszczyński refers to these same commandments as the seventh and eighth as is customary in the Catholic tradition.

26 Ibid, p. 108. Buszczyński has paraphrased selectively here and also replaced the words 'the currency, the tariff, and foreign policy' from the original by the Polish for 'duties, tariffs, domestic and foreign policy'.

27 Ibid, pp. 111–2. Buszczyński appears to have quoted very selectively here and inserted into the middle a sentence taken from the end of the original text, also misunderstanding its contextual meaning ('The difference between perjury and mendacity is not in the least one of morals or ethics. It is simply one of legal forms.').

28 Henry van Dyke, *The Spirit of America*, p. xv, The Macmillan Company, New York, 1912.

29 *Szkice Amerykańskie* is a series of reportage articles about America written by Henryk Sienkiewicz (winner of the Nobel prize for literature) who travelled around America in the late 1870s

30 Karl von Rotteck, *Allgemeine Geschichte vom Anfang der historischen Kenntniß bis auf unsere Zeiten: für denkende Geschichtsfreunde*, Vol. 9, p. 867, Herder, Freiburg, 1826.

31 Philarète Chasles, *Études sur les hommes et les mœurs au XIXe siècle*, Imprimerie de J. Claye et Ce, Paris, 1850, p. 309 '*Pendant que l'Europe se décompose, l'Amérique se forme.*' and p. 353 '*L'Amérique grandit; l'Europe s'en va!*'

32 Stefan Buszczyński, *Ameryka i Europa*, p. 155, Księgarnia Adolfa Dygasińskiego, Kraków, 1876.

33 Karl von Rotteck, *Allgemeine Geschichte vom Anfang der historischen Kenntniß bis auf unsere Zeiten: für denkende Geschichtsfreunde*, Vol. 9, pp. 868–9, Herder, Freiburg, 1826. Buszczyński appears to have quoted selectively from the passage at the end of the chapter.

34 Buszczyński makes a large number of factual errors in this chapter, including dates, names and details of historical events. They have not been individually noted or corrected but caution is recommended when relying on this information as a historical source.

35 Patrick Henry, speech at the Second Virginia Convention, St John's Church, Richmond, Virginia, 23 March 1775.

36 Declaration of Independence, 4 July 1776, Philadelphia, Pennsylvania.

37 Turgot, Baron de Laune, as quoted in *The Monthly Anthology, and Boston Review*, Vol. X, March 1811.

38 Phrase attributed to C.C. Pinckney.

39 President James Monroe's State of the Union Address to Congress in 1823. Only the words 'to extend their system' are a direct quotation; the remainder of Buszczyński's quotation appears to be a paraphrase.

40 President Jackson's Proclamation Regarding Nullification, 10 December 1832. This is not an accurate citation of the source: Buszczyński appears to have cobbled together a number of phrases from the proclamation.

41 A reference to Grant's decision to allow Confederate soldiers who owned their horses to take them home with them, as related in Chapter LXVII of *Personal Memoirs of U. S. Grant*, but it is not an exact quotation from these memoirs.

42 Stefan Buszczyński, *Rękopis z przyszłego wieku*, p. 43, Drukarnia „Głosu Narodu", Kraków, 1918.

www.ingramcontent.com/pod-product-compliance
Ingram Content Group UK Ltd.
Pitfield, Milton Keynes, MK11 3LW, UK
UKHW041956190726
13854UKWH00005B/2016

9 788395 556203